Speed Reading People

Analyzing Personality & Signs in Conversation -
How to Read, Understand,
Talk to & Influence People
(Effective Communication Training
Mastery to
Improve Your Social Skills)

Harvey Augustus

D1366492

© **Copyright 2020 - All rights reserved.**

This content is provided with the sole purpose of providing relevant information on a specific topic for which every reasonable effort has been made to ensure that it is both accurate and reasonable. Nevertheless, by purchasing this content you consent to the fact that the author, as well as the publisher, are in no way experts on the topics contained herein, regardless of any claims as such that may be made within. As such, any suggestions or recommendations that are made within are done so purely for entertainment value. It is recommended that you always consult a professional prior to undertaking any of the advice or techniques discussed within.

This is a legally binding declaration that is considered both valid and fair by both the Committee of Publishers Association and the American Bar Association and should be considered as legally binding within the United States.

The reproduction, transmission, and duplication of any of the content found herein, including any specific or extended information will be done as an illegal act regardless of the end form the information ultimately takes. This includes copied versions of the work both physical, digital and audio unless express consent of the Publisher is provided beforehand. Any additional rights reserved.

Furthermore, the information that can be found within the pages described forthwith shall be considered both accurate and truthful when it comes to the recounting of facts. As such, any use, correct or incorrect, of the provided information will render the Publisher free of responsibility as to the actions taken outside of their direct purview. Regardless, there are zero scenarios where the original author or the Publisher can be deemed liable in any fashion for any damages or hardships that may result from any of the information discussed herein.

Additionally, the information in the following pages is intended only for informational purposes and should thus be thought of as universal. As befitting its nature, it is presented without assurance regarding its prolonged validity or interim quality. Trademarks that are mentioned are done without written consent and can in no way be considered an endorsement from the trademark holder.

Table of Contents

Your Free Resource Is Awaiting

To better help you, I've created a simple mind map you can use *right away* to easily understand, quickly recall and readily use what you'll be learning in this book.

Click Here To Get Your Free Resource

Alternatively, here's the link:

https://viebooks.club/freeresourcemindmapforspeedreadingpeople

Your Free Resource Is Waiting..

Get Your Free Resource Now!

Introduction

Welcome to *Speed Reading People*. In this book, we will talk about what speed reading is, discover how it can help improve our interactions with others, and learn how to apply it in a variety of situations

Whether you are aware of it or not, you read people every single day. When you walk past a stranger on the sidewalk, you subconsciously judge if you believe they are safe or not. You decide if you should wave hello or not. When you get to work, you read your coworkers. You look at their emotions to see how they are feeling. You look at their movements to see if they are rushed or stressed. How you read them determines how you will interact with them.

Reading people is a skill that we do without trying, but it is something that we can do quickly and easily if we learn more about something called speed reading. Speed reading is the ability to take multiple people-reading strategies and apply them to the people we encounter in a quick and efficient way.

Throughout this book, we will study personal testimonies from speed reading experts as well as explore the scientific evidence behind this topic. Furthermore, we will go over this information in a practical way that allows you to apply the information to your own life, including exercises in each chapter to help you nurture your speed-reading skills. You will even get a glimpse at how I have used speed reading in my own life—past and present, personal and professional, and in cases involving my patients as a licensed professional counselor, or LPC.

If you are ready to read the people around you with great skill and interact with others in a whole new way, you have come to the right place. I am so happy to take you on this speed-reading journey and can't wait to help show you the tips and tricks you need to see success!

See you on the inside.

Chapter 1: What Is Speed Reading and Why You Should Learn How To Do It

Imagine you are in a store and you need help finding a product. You look around you and see four different employees. One employee is a teenage boy. He is staring at his phone. This makes you believe he is not interested in his job or that he does not take his work seriously. Because of this, he might not be the right person to help you. The next employee that you see is wearing a button-down, collared shirt with a tie. He is wearing dress pants and shiny black shoes as well. He is pacing up and down an aisle while talking into an earpiece. He seems busy and like he might be the store manager, so he might not be the person to ask, either.

The third employee is about to head to the back. They might be taking off their work vest and talking about how hungry they are. Since they are heading to a break, they are probably not going to help you right now, either. Next, you see a woman standing near a shelf straightening the products.

She is focused on what she is doing and gives a friendly smile to the customers who walk by her. You decide that she will be the person to help you find what you are looking for.

In this situation, whether you were aware of it or not, you were reading the people around you. You were looking to find the person who would be able to best assist you based on what they looked like, what activities they were partaking in, and the emotions they were showing. Based on these judgements, you narrowed down your options and chose the "best" employee for the job.

With this example, it is easy to see that reading people is actually something that we do every day. Speed reading people is similar to this; it's just a specific way to read people. It is purposeful, quick, and efficient. It helps you to read the people around you in a way that betters your life and helps you to get the things you need in just about any situation.

Speed reading involves many aspects. It can be practiced if you only know one or two of these pieces, but the more that you know, the more effective your readings will be. Some of the things that speed reading is based on are how a person looks and dresses, emotional intelligence, personality types, character, body language, employment, and social status.

It is also important to note that reading people is both a conscious and subconscious act. There are times that we judge people without trying to and without even realizing what we are doing. This is human nature and is simply how we are wired to behave. Conscious reading includes the ways that you can learn to read people better. These acts are focused and purposeful. They do not replace our subconscious judgements, as those are always in the back of our minds. They can, however, add to our ability to read people tremendously.

So now that we have a basic understanding of what speed reading is, why should you learn how to do it? Basically, I believe that you should learn to speed read the people around you because it will benefit your life in many areas. Speed reading can help you get along with your coworkers, understand your bosses, and train new employees well. Speed reading people can help you in all relationships from familial to romantic. It can help you talk to strangers. It can keep you safe in dangerous situations. It can basically help you get what you want from most of the people that you surround yourself with.

Speed reading takes an ability that you are born with and multiplies it so that it can be an extremely beneficial tool in your life. It makes sense of the subconscious readings you do of the people around you. It helps you to better understand not only the people closest to you and the random strangers in your life but also more and more of yourself.

There are situations where speed reading can help you in your life that are like the example we used from the store, and there are times when it can help you in much larger ways as well. Speed reading can help you get the job of your dreams. It can even help you meet the love of your life.

Overall, it is a skill that can help you in every area of your life that involves others. It adds to your subconscious ability to read people. It helps you to get the things you need from the relationships in your life. The more you learn about speed reading, the more it can add to your life in positive ways.

Chapter 2: Personality Versus Character

One of the main things that you judge people for is their personality. The personality of friends and coworkers allows you to decide if you have enough similarities to get along. The personality of strangers is one of the first things you notice when you talk to them as well as one of the most memorable things about them. Let's start by looking into what personality is.

Personality is defined as the mixture of traits that makes a person who they are. It is something unique. No two people on Earth have the same exact personality. It is something that people are aware of. It can be shaped by life experiences, likes, and dislikes, and wants and needs. It can be formed by who the person wants to be as well. It can change daily if the person wants it to.

But now you may ask how this is different from character?

Character is who a person is at the core. It is often shaped by the life that the person has lived. It includes their morals and beliefs. It is the thing that shows when a person is going through a challenge.

Character and personality are two different aspects of the person. Understanding this can help us to better ready those around us. Why? Because once you understand the difference between the two, you'll be able to spot both a person's personality and a person's character. This will help you in your speed-reading quest.

These differences come from a source called the 100 Steps Mission. This site is run by Natalie Hol, author of *The 100 Steps to Financial Independence: Your Definitive Roadmap to Achieving Your Financial Dreams*. On her site, Hol speaks not only about finances and how to take charge of your financial future but also about inspirational leadership, how to use your knowledge about others, and what you can glean from being around them to your advantage. It is a resource for leadership development, which I already know is greatly improved with the ability to read those around you.

Techniques Versus Principles

Personality is based on techniques. It is based on the ways in which a person lives, how they talk, and how they act. It's based on how they joke and laugh as well as how they behave in front of a crowd of strangers versus with a close friend.

Character, on the other hand, is based on principles. It is the reason why a person behaves the way that they do. If a person's personality is kind, it might be because of the beliefs that their character holds, for example. It involves a person's morals, values, and principles.

"Appear To Be" Versus "Actually Be"

Personality is based on "Appear To Be." This means that personality can be seen through a judgement. It can also be based on how a person portrays themselves and not how they actually feel. For example, a person can portray themselves as an outgoing individual. They can speak loudly, talk to everyone around them, and display a level of confidence that is hard to match for the people around them. Deep down, however, they could be very harsh on themselves and have low self-esteem. They could wish they were staying at home rather than spending time surrounded by people. Personality shows what a person lets us see. It might not always show the truth behind who the person actually is.

Character is based on "Actually Be." A person's character is who they really are. It includes the things they feel deep down in their soul. It is not something that people can change purposefully throughout their lives. It can only change if a person goes through an event that truly shapes who they are. If you see a person's character, you see the person that they truly are. It's something that you can always trust and believe in.

What Personality Revolves Around Versus What Character Revolves Around

We have already seen why personality and character are so different, but these details really add a depth to the differences between the two. For starters, personality revolves around an image that a person creates for themselves. It is how a person wants to be seen by the people around them, and it is self-created.

It revolves around how a person acts when they are around others. It shows if a person is friendly and talkative or submissive and shy. It includes how a person talks and laughs, what they talk about, and even how they move around in public.

It even involves how the person manages both the people around them and the things that they see on a daily basis. Are they strong leaders with a belief that they are at a higher standard than those around them, or do they consider their employees as equals? Do they avoid challenges, or do they jump right in? Do they complain or stay positive?

Character shows just about the opposite of all these descriptions. It revolves not around an image that a person creates for themselves but around integrity and who a person truly is.

Character can show us a lot about a person and their moral code, even if they barely speak a word to us. Character is more about whether we will help those around us, even if there is no benefit to us, if we speak out against injustice, and whether we would have courage in tough situations.

It is important to note that personality might be the first thing you notice about a person, but it is usually not the most important thing that you should be looking for. You can tell a certain amount about a person through their personality, but if you really want to read them well, you will need to look into their character.

When reading people for their personality and character, you will likely see their personality show through on everyday tasks. It is important to know that this may be the person they want you to see and not the person who they really are.

You will typically see the character when a person is being challenged. If they see something they do not believe is right, their character might show through. It also might show through if they are going through a tough time in their life. If you see a person's character, you should believe what you see. It is who they truly are. If you are lucky enough to see a person's character, use it. It will help you to read them well.

Fill out the worksheet below to see if you can tell the differences between personality and character. Place the letter "P" next to things that refer to personality and "C" next to those that refer to the character. The answers are listed on the next page.

Personality or Character?

1. A man talking loudly in a group of friends.

2. A woman waving to every person she passes on the sidewalk.

3. A girl taking responsibility for the mistake she made at work.

4. A boy fighting to make sure his female coworkers have equal pay.

5. A man telling jokes to his children.

6. A woman always wearing name brand clothing.

Worksheet Answers:

1. P

2. P

3. C

4. C

5. P

6. P

Chapter 3: What Causes Specific Personality Traits

Now that we know what exactly personality is, let's look into how it comes to be. Personality is a complex part of who we are, and it is made up of many different factors. Without our personality, we would all be a blank slate. Our personality tells us, and others, more about us.

First, let's look at one of the places where our personality could have started — our genes. This information is based on Daniel Nettle's article "The Science Behind Personality". Scientists have done many studies and recently found that certain personality traits, like being an introvert or an extrovert, could be genetic. They believe that this trait is genetic because of a specific gene that codes the dopamine in our brains. The gene decides how long the sequence of this neurotransmitter is and the length of the sequence affects whether a person becomes an introvert or an extrovert.

Scientists also believe that parts of the personality come from the theory of evolution. They believe this because many animals have unique personalities. It is not just something for humans. It also adds to why the theory of natural selection makes sense because personality makes every living being unique from one another.

Psychologists today state that our personality comes from three basic needs that we all have as humans. In her article, "From Needs to Goals and Representations: Foundations for a Unified Theory of Motivation, Personality, and Development", psychologist Carol Dweck asserts that these three basic needs consist of our need to protect the world we live in, our need to act on this world competently, and our need to be accepted by the people around us.

Dweck also states that as we reach these three basic needs, we start to form feelings and opinions about the world that we live in. These feelings are based on beliefs, emotion, and action tenancies (BEATs).

We are all made up of these three basic needs and the beliefs, action tenancies, and emotion that goes along with them. When we really start to form our own personalities and stand out from the people around us is when we start to make conscious and subconscious goals based on the three needs and BEATs.

Let's look into some examples of this. If we feel deeply about our need to protect the world we live in by means of protecting the Earth itself, we would begin to make environmental goals. We might pick up trash from the ground every time we see it outside. We might use reusable or compostable plates, cups, and utensils every time we eat. We might even advocate for these things to our friends and acquaintances every chance we get. This belief and the resulting actions become a part of our personality.

Next, let's say we feel strongly about the third of the three basic needs, needing to feel accepted by the people around us. Because of this, we make it our goal to make friends with every person in our workplace. To do this, we smile often. We might talk to people every chance we get. We might even talk loudly or laugh often for people to notice us better and have a better chance of wanting to become our friends. These actions create a personality trait in us that is friendly and outgoing.

We've looked into the scientific explanations for where our personality comes from. Next, let's look into the things in our daily life that help to shape our personality as well.

The things you participate in throughout your life can affect the person you turn out to be as well. For example, your personality might change after you graduate from college simply because you have gained so much knowledge and created new goals for yourself. It might even change after you graduate from an added boost of self-esteem.

Your personality might change based on the people whom you spend the most time with as well. If you see someone every day and like who they are, you might begin to act more like them. You could do this consciously or subconsciously, but either way, it could affect the person you portray yourself as. That is why you will hear parents worry about the influence that their children's friends have on them; their company really can change the child's personality if they hang around a strong enough influence.

Personalities can even shift based on what situation you are in at the time. If you are at work, you might act more reserved and professional. If you are at home, you might act more laid back and relaxed. If you are out with friends, you might act more comical and outgoing.

Overall, it is clear that our personalities are shaped by many different occurrences. They are first shaped by our genetic make-up. They are then shaped by our psychological needs as well as the beliefs and actions that come from these needs. Lastly, they are shaped by the lives we live and the people we strive to be. Personalities are complex and ever-changing. When we learn more about our personalities, we can learn so much more about ourselves.

Let's do another exercise to better understand where our personalities come from. In the spaces below, consider each of the personality traits and write down some of your thoughts on each one.

Where Do These Traits Come From?

Extroversion:

_____

Friendliness:

_____

Environmentalism:

_____

Confidence:

_____

Chapter 4: Each Personality Type Described

Now that we have identified exactly what personality is and where it comes from, we will explore the different types of personality traits. This is where our speed reading focus starts to come into play. If you have a deep understanding of each of the following personality traits, you will be able to read the people around you more quickly and easily. The personality types in this chapter will be broken up into sections. There are many different theories on how personalities are grouped, and it is important to understand them all in order to speed read people efficiently.

Am I An Introvert Or An Extrovert?

There are several types of personality tests that can group people into categories to explain what type of person they are. Each personality test is different, but most are made up of four categories. In each category, there are two personalities. When you take the test, you are given one letter from each category that best describes who you are. The result of the test is then a string of four letters. It is known to accurately describe a person's personality and is used in many professional and personal settings worldwide. This particular personality test has become so popular that some people even take simplified variations of it online as fun quizzes through such social media outlets as Facebook. Despite this trivialization, the results are still valid and very useful when it comes to speed reading others and understanding your own personality.

Many people like to use these tests to help them figure out whether they are an introvert or an extrovert naturally. Taking a test that includes this kind of section can help you figure out whether you will feel recharged with some alone time or if social activities are more your style.

Here are some ways that you can tell if a person is introverted or extroverted:

Introvert:

- Speaks calmly

- Withdraws from the center of attention

- Does not talk much

- Stays on one topic for a long period of time

- Has only a few close friends

- Might talk quietly and slowly

Extrovert:

- Enthusiastic

- Loves to be the center of attention

- Talks a lot

- Brings up many brief conversation topics in a short time

- Friends with everyone

- Talks loudly and quickly

As you can see, these personality traits are quite a bit different, and knowing which one you are can influence how you interact with the world around you.

The next section of these kinds of tests will include Sensor versus Intuitive. Most people in the world are sensors as only about one-third of the population tests out to be intuitive. Because of this, if you are unable to tell, it might be best to read the person you are speaking to as a sensor. Sensors talk more about concrete details that are able to be seen while intuitives are more creative and idealistic.

Here are some ways that you can tell if a person is a Sensor or an Intuitive:

Sensor:

- Looks for facts

- Realistic

- Practical

- Focuses on the past and present

- Explores with the five senses

- Bases information off of experiences

Intuitive:

- Creates new ideas

- Dreams

- Theoretical

- Imaginative

- Focuses on the future

- Creates visions

The next section might consist of Thinker versus Feeler. More often than not, men are thinkers and women are feelers. However, for one-third of the population, this is the opposite. Because of this, if you are absolutely unable to tell if a person is a thinker or a feeler, you could assume that if they are a man, they are a thinker and if they are a woman, they are a feeler. However, there are times when this will not be accurate.

Thinkers are confident. They do not take it personally if you disagree with them, and they are good at coming to agreements rather than arguing over what they would see as trivial things. They stand for truth and justice. They make goals for themselves and reach them.

Feelers are much different. Feelers believe that it is more important to help others than to better themselves. Feelers are friendly and kind. They will speak about their personal lives and their feelings instead of concrete topics. They value love and peace and the people around them.

Here are some ways you can tell if a person is a thinker or a feeler:

Thinker:

- Logical

- Seeks justice and truth

- Judges others

- Goal setting and reaching

- Honest

Feeler:

- Values love and peace

- Personal

- Loves the people around them

- Friendly

- Helps others before themselves

The last part of these kinds of tests include Judger versus Perceiver. Judgers make up the larger part of the world's population. They are serious and often maintain a strict schedule. They are organized, like to have a plan, and like to be in control. They are good at time management but tend to always be rushing because of this.

Perceivers, on the other hand, are almost the opposite. They are spontaneous, and organization is not their strong suit. They are flexible, open, and do not always need to stick to the plan. They can be procrastinators because of this and might struggle with time management. However, there are many great points to their personality as well. They do not need everything to be perfect and just kind of go with the flow.

Here are some things that can help you determine if a person is a perceiver or a judger:

Judger:

- Serious

- Sticks to a schedule

- Clean and organized

- Leaders

Perceiver:

- Open and light-hearted

- Spontaneous

- Messy and unorganized

- Goes with the flow

Perceivers are given the letter P in the last section of their sequence and Judgers are given the letter J.

Personality Types #1

Now we need to put these parts together and figure out which personality we are. This is not only going to be helpful in letting us understand ourselves better but can be a great way to make speed reading a little bit easier. Furthermore, it is great practice for when we try and apply this same method to speed reading others.

Remember, the different parts of your personality according to this test do not have any influence over the other parts of your personality. Whether you are a judger or a perceiver does not influence whether you are an introvert or an extrovert or vice versa. You can be an introverted judger or an extroverted judger, for example. Even if two or more of your personality traits seem contradictory, they can still work together to describe your true personality. Humans are, after all, very complex creatures.

To help guide you through determining someone's four personality traits as explained by this personality test, I will be comparing my personality as determined by this personality test with my sister's personality.

As previously stated, the first part of your personality will determine whether you recharge when you are out with people, being part of a social group, or if your recharging takes place at home alone with a good book. The best way to tell if you are an introvert or an extrovert includes the following:

Extrovert:

- Energy is directed to the people around them

- Notices and remembers social happenings

- Bases decisions on views of others

- Comfortable in social settings

- Motivated by and craves interaction

- Dark side could be overconfidence

Introvert:

- Energy is directed inward

- Remembers thoughts and feelings

- Bases decision on their own needs

- Comfortable with close friends

- Motivated by and craves alone time

- Dark side could be excluding themselves

Given these traits, I would be considered an extrovert. I am most comfortable among many friends and acquaintances in social settings and have no problems approaching strangers and making friends out of them. I often hate to be alone as well and get restless when I don't get the interaction that I crave. My sister would argue that I also show signs of the dark side of extroverts, i.e. overconfidence.

My sister, though, is an introvert. She hates going out with more than just a few close friends and would rather spend her Saturdays at home watching movies with her dogs than attending parties. I have noticed that she tends to isolate herself and exclude herself from most social functions, but she appears happier that way.

The second part of your personality helps to determine how you interact with and process the world. Sensors process things from a more realistic standpoint, whereas intuitives lean more toward creativity and idealism. The following are the best indicators as to whether you are a sensor or an intuitive:

Sensor:

- Energy is directed toward realism

- Notices and remembers facts and evidence

- Focused cognitive function

- Needs to experience things firsthand

- Motivated by proof

Intuitive:

- Energy is directed to creativity

- Motivated by new ideas

- Makes conclusions creatively

- Comfortable in an open and accepting environment

- Dark side could be ignoring the facts

My sister and I are both sensors. We pay more attention to facts and statistics and make all our conclusions based on those. We also tend to need to experience things firsthand in order to believe them, which can often serve as a point of contention between us and a couple of our friends who are more creative and intuitive. If you have never seen a sensor and an intuitive get into a discussion about the paranormal, I highly do not recommend it—things will get heated.

The third personality trait will tell you how you think and what really motivates you in life. It tells you whether you are more logical or emotional and if you are more motivated by your personal goals or by what you and others are feeling. The most prominent ways to identify if someone is a thinker or a feeler are:

Thinker:

- Motivated by goals

- Energy is directed toward truth and justice

- Sets cognitive goals

- Notices and remembers logic

Feeler:

- Energy is directed toward helping others

- Notices emotional side of things

- Focused on love and peace

- Needs personal interaction

- Motivated by feelings

Again, this is an area in which my sister and I diverge. My sister is more of a thinker, whereas I am a feeler. She is entirely motivated by the goals she sets and always makes sure that truth and justice prevails. It made growing up with her very interesting, considering that she made certain that I never got away with anything. She is also more logical than I am, trying to solve problems in a practical way rather than putting people's emotions first. I, on the other hand, always put people's emotions ahead of every other element of a problem. I'm more motivated by what I feel and pursue whatever satisfies those feelings at the moment, regardless of what goals I've set. I prefer to show compassion and not rock the boat, even if it means bending the truth or slacking off in the justice area. This has helped me to be successful in helping others, while my sister's thinker trait makes her a great lawyer.

The final category in this four-part personality test lets you know if you are organized or more organized chaos. Judgers, well, judge and organize, while perceivers are a bit looser and more free spirits that go with the flow. The tell-tale differences between these kinds of personality traits are:

Judger:

- Serious cognitive function

- Motivated by schedules

- Needs organization

- Dark side could be judging others

Perceiver

- Open-minded cognitive function

- Motivated by opportunity

- Needs to be spontaneous

- Dark side could be disorganization

With these definitions, I would probably be considered a perceiver. I grab at whatever opportunity comes my way, even if it doesn't fit into my pre-determined schedule. In fact, I use the term "schedule" fairly loosely as I mostly just write down the deadlines and appointments I absolutely must meet and then let whatever else happens happen. While I look well put together, I also dress casually whenever I can, getting away with business casual if I can't just wear my favorite pair of 501s and a t-shirt. (At least this puts my patients more at ease than some stiff in a suit.) My office is very neat and tidy so that my patients will trust me to help them and talk with me. However, things at home are an entirely different story. My sister and my partner both call me a "black hole"—my personal space is so disorganized that almost anything that enters my apartment seems to disappear into the cosmos.

My sister, in contrast, is a judger. She sets strict schedules and sticks to them. She's so attached to them and so set on having her personal space stay exactly the way she's put it that our family has often wondered if she's borderline OCD. Really, though, it's just a part of her personality. She can also be a bit judgmental, especially towards disorganized people, but it always comes from a place of trying to help people be their best.

Knowing your own personality type and really exploring who you are as a person will make it much easier for you to figure out which style you can use to speed read. No one is going to learn in the same manner, and working to understand your style and what clicks with you can be so much easier when you know more about your personality type!

Personality Types #2

There are a few different methods you can use to determine your personality type and figure out more about yourself. If you feel like the one above didn't seem to work the best for your needs or didn't really describe the person you are, then maybe this one is a better option.

This one is going to be split up into several categories. The point of these categories is to really distinguish the differences in the personalities while not focusing on one type over another. It is so effective at helping us understand how a person behaves and their motivation that many employers use it to help them with team building and more. Let's look at some of the different categories that come here.

Dominance

The first personality trait is dominance. If someone is dominant, they are described as a person who is direct, determined, and decisive.

Influence

The next trait is influence. It is described as interactive, involved, imaginative, and influencing.

Steadiness

Then there is steadiness. It is described as sweet, steady, and stable.

Conscientious

Finally, we have conscientious. It is described as calculating, cautious, contemplative, and competent.

As I mentioned earlier, when you take this test, you will likely match up with exactly two of the personality types. You could match with only one, with three, or with all four, but it is extremely rare. This means that when you use this personality tool to speed read the people around you, they will likely fit into two of the categories listed above.

Let's study these categories in a little more detail:

Dominance

- Needs to be respected and be in control

- Wants to have choices

Influence

- Needs to be known and recognized

- Wants to be liked

Steadiness

- Needs the approval of others

- Wants to feel appreciated

Conscientious

- Needs to follow values

- Wants to be successful

Like with the first personality test, I will evaluate my sister and myself to help you see how these personality traits might play out in different people. Neither of us fully fit into any of these categories, which makes the previous test much more accurate for both of us, but we do have two categories each that match us closest. For me, those traits are influence and steadiness. I do want to be liked and appreciated, and it puts a spring in my step to be recognized when I go out and see people I have met through friends and at parties. I would like to think that I do not *need* the approval of others, and I do not necessarily go out of my way to get people's approval. However, I do seriously take other people's feelings and opinions into account whenever I do anything, and it makes me feel better about my decisions when other people agree with me.

My sister, though, drifts more toward dominance and being conscientious. Because she likes to be very organized, she has a strong need to be in control. She has specific values that she must follow, including her pursuit of truth and justice, and strives hard to succeed at every goal she sets for herself. While she enjoys the respect that she gets as a lawyer, she does not necessarily need it, so that might be where this particular trait fails to describe her. However, she does hate when she is not given choices in any given matter; she likes to plan everything out for herself, so choices are crucial.

As I said, neither of us are entirely described by the traits associated with this test, so readings of my sister and myself are probably more accurate when someone uses the previous test. Nevertheless, these traits give a rough idea of who we are as people, and this gives whoever is speed reading us an advantage.

Highly Sensitive People Versus Normal People

This type of personality trait is based on one type of personality: the highly sensitive person. This type of person is not like most of us. They work differently than others, think differently than others, love differently than others, and simply feel differently than the people around them.

Highly sensitive people are exactly what their name depicts them to be. They are more sensitive than others to almost everything. They are not only extremely aware of their emotions, but they also do not like loud noises, for example. They think things through at a deeper and more meaningful level than the rest of us.

Highly sensitive people are fairly rare. Only about one-fifth of the people in the world have this unique personality trait. I have only ever known one or two highly sensitive people in my life, and they have been a couple of the kindest—if most emotional—people I have had the pleasure of meeting. To find out if you are a highly sensitive person, you can take a test that was created by the psychologist who discovered the personality type.

Here are some personality traits of highly sensitive people:

- Intuitive

- Prefer to work alone

- Kind

- Easily irritated

- Amplified emotional reactions

- Easily offended

Another interesting note about people who are highly sensitive is that most are introverted but not all. About seventy percent of highly sensitive people are introverts, and about thirty percent are extroverted.

This is interesting because many of the introvert characteristics line up with the highly sensitive person characteristics. If you are speed reading a person who is both extroverted and highly sensitive, this is an important thing to note. They could seem both introverted and extroverted because of their characteristics, but some traits might come from being highly sensitive instead.

We have gone over the characteristics of people who are highly sensitive, but we still need to look into the characteristics of the people who are not highly sensitive. We will refer to these people as "normal" during this segment, though I know that all people are normal people. I am simply noting the difference between people who are highly sensitive and people who are not more sensitive than normal.

People who are not overly sensitive, or normal people, do not show any of the signs of highly sensitive people. Normal people will cry with certain circumstances but usually will not cry during the middle of the workday, for example.

Normal people might not be as intuitive as highly sensitive people. Intuition is something that everyone has, so you might still notice it in normal people, but it will not be extremely accurate and noticeable like it is in the minds of the highly sensitive.

Normal people will also have an overall calm demeanor and response system. For example, we mentioned the fact that highly sensitive people can easily become irritated. We also mentioned that highly sensitive people can become easily offended.

Normal people will have a more typical reaction to adversity. If a person asks them to go over a project one more time because it has a few small errors, they will understand. They will not think automatically that the person who asked the question was being mean. They will not go straight to believing that they are bad at their job after one small misstep.

When normal people become upset, they will have normal reactions. For example, they will not cry and withdraw themselves from their friends just because they said something that someone else did not agree with at a social gathering, whereas an overly sensitive person might act in a way similar to this.

Normal people also do not prefer to work alone all of the time. This is a tricky characteristic because it can mean a few different things. For example, if a person loves to be alone, they might be introverted and gaining back their energy from their alone time. They might also be overly sensitive and deep in thought during their alone time. If a person loves being the center of attention, they might be extroverted, or they might not be highly sensitive at all. These things are not guaranteed, however.

If a person loves to be alone, you will need to figure out if they are introverted or if they are highly sensitive. You can do this by looking into all of the characteristics of each of these two personality types. The person could be introverted, highly sensitive, or even both.

If a person loves to be around others, you can do the same thing to figure out if they are extroverted or if they are simply not highly sensitive. Again, they could be one, the other, or both, but they do not have to be both.

Another important thing to remember when trying to figure out if someone is a highly sensitive person or if they are a normal person is that only about twenty percent of the world's population are highly sensitive people. Because of this, there is a better chance that you are talking to a normal person versus someone who is highly sensitive. You might even want to begin by assuming that the person who you are speed reading is normal unless they start to show the signs of being overly sensitive since there is such a large chance that they are in fact normal.

You might even meet someone someday who is less sensitive than most of the people that you meet. They might, for example, speak in a way that some people refer to as speaking without a filter. This means they will say anything that comes into their mind whether it is kind or cruel. These less-sensitive people might never become upset or seem to even notice when they are being judged or criticized. They might talk about topics that others do not want to hear. They might talk loudly and to everyone in a room without ever shying away. They might seem rude or not seem to show emotion, even when things in their life become extremely challenging.

I remember working with a patient one time who struggled with this. She didn't understand why she was having trouble keeping friends and suffered from low self-esteem because it seemed like no one wanted to be around her. She was a very social and lovely person, and it took me some time to figure out what the problem was.

She had a horrible time with that filter. She said things as she saw them, which could be an admirable quality, but at times, it could take things too far. This landed her in trouble and often made others mad at her.

At the time, she had come to me because of problems at work. Her boss had been giving her work that was outside of the job description, and she just didn't have time to handle it. While I didn't expect her to just sit back and take it, yelling at the boss and calling him names and getting into an altercation was probably not the best idea, either. During our time together, we learned proper ways to talk about how we felt with a bit of a filter added on. When she was done with her sessions, my patient realized that when the workload was too much or wasn't her job, bringing it up respectfully with her boss could get her so much further.

People who are not very sensitive at all might have gone through something difficult in their life and let go of their sensitivity to cope with that difficult thing. This is important to know when reading people so you can have an idea of where this person's behaviors could be stemming from. It is also important to know so that you can see deeper into who the person truly is and what their background and past might have been like.

These people might not have gone through something difficult though, and a low level of sensitivity might just be a part of their personality. This is not at all a bad thing; it is simply just a piece of who they are. It's something that sets them apart from others and turns them into the person who they are supposed to be.

Sensitive people see the world differently than the rest of us. They are more attuned to what others are feeling or thinking, and they like to keep this in mind with any actions they use. Reading them can add in a new challenge, because they often feel the emotions of those around them as their own. Understanding how this will affect others can make a difference in how you speed read someone and gives us a good example of how everyone is different.

How People Feel and Give Love

Another personality tool that you can use while speed reading the people around you is how they feel and give love. Understanding how those around you feel and give love—and how you do so—can enrich not only your romantic relationships but also your friendships and family ties. Even your relationships with your coworkers can be strengthened by using this personality tool as you learn how best to show your appreciation for them.

It is important to note that when you are reading people, they most likely receive love in only one way. However, some people can express love through multiple methods. Some might also receive love one way and express it in another. There are others still who did not grow up in a loving environment and so do not know how to receive or give love because they did not learn how to feel loved when they were young.

The ways in which we feel and give love fall under five categories: words of affirmation, acts of service, receiving gifts, quality time, and physical touch.

Words of affirmation involve hearing good things. People who prefer words of affirmation like compliments. They appreciate it when the people around them tell them that they love them or that they did a good job. This kind of person might seek attention or compliments, and they might perform better in relationships and jobs when they are spoken to kindly.

Acts of service are when people do nice things for each other. For example, they might feel loved best when their significant other shovels the snow off their car for them in the cold mornings before work. They might also like it when their coworkers help them with a big job when they know they are overwhelmed.

Receiving gifts is exactly what it sounds like. These people might love when their husband brings home flowers or when their boss drops off a treat after they have had a successful week (or a hard week). I have always been one to feel and express love this way. I never understood why, but receiving gifts from the people I am closest to has always made me feel loved and appreciated. Similarly, giving gifts to the people I love feels like the best way that I can show them how much they mean to me. After all, the right gift shows just how much someone knows and pays attention to someone else, so it feels like the perfect way to express love for another person.

The fourth category is quality time. These people do not want physical things most of the time. They simply want to enjoy time with the people around them. They might appreciate an afternoon walk with their partner or love it if their favorite coworker invited them out for lunch. As I found out later in our relationship, my current partner prefers to receive love through quality time. To them, there is no better way to show your love for someone than to just be there for them, talk to them, and get involved in their life.

The final category is physical touch. These people feel the most love when they are able to feel another person's touch. They might like to cuddle at home, or they might even appreciate a simple high five at work. Despite being an introvert, my sister falls under this category. She does not like to be touched by many people, so physical touch is the ultimate expression of intimacy to her. Even if it's just a close friend or family member giving her a quick hug after a long day, she never feels more loved than when someone she loves physically touches her.

As you can see, how we give and feel love can be used in many ways and not just in romantic relationships. If you are speed reading people with this personality tool in mind, you could pay attention to the things that they like as you try them. You could also listen to them talk and see if they mention any of these applications more than others. Also, you could pay attention to how they express their love. Do they give out gift cards for every birthday and Christmas? If so, they might show and feel love by giving gifts. Do they hug everyone they meet? If so, they might prefer physical touch.

In your speed-reading process, you should also learn your preferred expressions of love. If you pay attention to this and allow it to benefit your life, you might be able to better see how others like to give and take love at home, at work, at school, and in your everyday life.

How Different Personalities See the World

With all the different types of personalities out there, we must understand that each person sees the world in a different way. If you are an extrovert, you enjoy going out and being with friends and in social groups and find being at home and relaxing a bit unnerving. The introvert, on the other hand, likes to be around others but would find going out every night to be exhausting.

One personality type is not necessarily better than another, but they view the world differently. And that was just an example of one part of the personality! Imagine what happens when we add perceiver, judger, and sensitive into the mix!

Based on your personality type, you might respond to things that happen in the world in different manners. One example of this is words of praise. Some people seem to not care less if they are praised for their work or not. They head into work each day and try to do the best they can, and they are proud of a job well done. Then there are those who, even though they know they did a good job, crave the praise. Without this, they will feel left behind or that something is wrong with the work they did.

If you find that you meet someone who needs this praise and words of affirmation, then you can never overdo it with the amount of praise you give. They thrive on hearing that you appreciate them, that you notice their hard work, and that you value them. Failure to do this, even if unintentional, can sometimes make the other person worry, and can cause a rift in the relationship, even if you did not mean it.

This is just one example of how someone can see the world differently than you. You might like the praise but not see it as important. Someone else might see the praise as unnecessary and bothersome. And still others need that praise to make them feel good.

Acts of service or helping others can be another personality trait to watch for. If you notice that someone is always helping to pick up after you, offers to run an errand, will stay late and work with you, or folds your clothes in a special way you like, then this is likely how they view showing kindness and love for others. When you do small acts of kindness for them back, this can make them over-the-moon happy.

Have you ever been around that person who seems to love to give and receive gifts? It doesn't have to even be Christmas. They will pick up something thoughtful they saw at the store for you, and they seem to get so much delight any time that they can provide a small token to some-one else. It goes the other way as well. They are more than pleased any time you think of them with a gift, no matter how big or small.

One person might just enjoy your time and atten-tion and will feel that you taking a day off and spending it with them or putting your work away early can be the best thing in the world, while the gifts and praise doesn't mean as much.

Physical touch is another thing to pay attention to. Some people don't want to be touched unless they are really familiar with you. Others feel that touch is the best way for them to communicate with one another.

Can you imagine how all these different types of people and different types of personalities are going to see the world differently? What is important to someone else may not seem like a big deal to you, but what is important to you may not be a big deal to someone else.

This is a long list of personality types, but if we have an organized system, it is easy and efficient to use them when we are speed reading the people around us. The first system that you can try when you are reading people is to simply know this information.

If you know the different personality types and their characteristics, the people that have these personality types may stand out to you. For example, if you know that introverted people tend to be quiet and like alone time and you meet someone who matches these criteria, you will recognize right away that they are an introvert without even trying. If you know the information well, it will show up in your mind when you need it the most.

Another system that you could use would be to run through the personality categories one by one in your mind. To do this, you might want to organize the categories into a list in your thoughts so that you will know where to start and so that you do not forget about any of the categories.

With these personality traits, you can discover so much about who a person truly is. You can see where the person's energy is directed, you can see what types of information the person tends to notice and remember, and you can even see how the person reaches conclusions and makes decisions. You can see the type of environment that the person is the most comfortable in. You can see the person's cognitive function and what they want and need in their life. You can see what they are happy with as well as what types of things can motivate them. You can see how they tick, and you can even see their potential dark sides.

Becoming familiar with the different types of personality tests that are out there, and exploring how to tell which kind of person fits into each one is going to make a big difference in how you are able to handle the different people you encounter in your life.

Remember that not everyone is going to fit into a nice little box. You can do all the personality tests that you would like, but you might find that someone is mostly introverted but have a bit of extrovert in them. Someone might be a bit dominant, but they aren't as rough and tough about it as they might seem.

For example, while my sister is introverted, it does not mean that she will avoid being around people at all costs or that she will not talk with people once she does get out. In fact, she can be quite the chatterbox once you get her started. The key is to just hit on a subject that she wants to talk about and feels comfortable with, and you would swear that she was actually a hyper-energetic extrovert. Sometimes all it takes to see another side of someone like that is to get them more comfortable with you, and then you will see their true, if conflicting, personalities.

On the other hand, just because I am more extroverted does not mean that I need to be around people all day, every day. Yes, I more often enjoy being around a bunch other people than I do just sitting at home by myself or with a couple of close friends. Still, there are times when I need some "me time" in order to get some rest and be ready for the next big get-together. After all, I am a feeler as well. I am more emotional—although not highly sensitive—and sometimes need a break from the highs and lows of other people's lives. I do not take myself out of the public eye for long, mind you, but I still need some me time to avoid the risk of social burnout. There are varying degrees of different personality traits and types, and it takes time to learn how to recognize each one.

People don't fit into little boxes that you create. They are varied and they will act how they want, regardless of what a personality test says. However, this is a good way to get an idea of how a certain person is going to react in different situations, and you can work from there as you get more experience with speed reading others.

Overall, it is easy to see that by speed reading a person's personality, we can learn a significant amount of information about them personally and about their lives. After reading through this information, you should take the tools above and use them to help you speed read others.

Chapter 5: How To Tell A Person's Personality Type

First, let's look at what you can learn from a person's appearance. The first thing that you might notice is if a person takes care of themselves well or not. If a person cares for themselves well, they will be in clean clothes and will practice basic hygiene techniques. For example, their hair and teeth will probably be brushed. They will be wearing nice, clean clothes as well.

Another thing that you might notice based on a person's appearance is how confident they are with themselves. If they are slouching or not making eye contact with the people around them, they might either be uncomfortable or not confident with themselves in the situation that they are in. This could point to them either being introverted or highly sensitive. You will be able to tell which based on the other traits that you notice in them.

You might also notice a person's vocabulary once you begin talking to them or even as you hear them speaking across the room. If a person uses large and sophisticated words, education might be important to them or they might be trying to sound professional for their job. Their vocabulary can also help you fit them into certain personality categories. If they talk a lot and use a large number of words, they might be extroverted, and you can pretty easily assume that they are normal and not highly sensitive. If they continue to talk positively to the people around them, you might be able to make the assumption that they respond best to positive words and praise.

Next, you might be able to learn more about the personality of the person that you are speed reading based on their occupation. If they have a job where they have to speak in front of large crowds or talk to clients for the entire day and they seem to love it, they are probably extroverted. If they are a counselor who loves to talk with clients about their feelings and mental health, you might be able to assume that they are highly sensitive or that they are more feeling versus thinking. If they lead a large company, you might be able to tell that they lean toward dominance on some of these personality tools.

Another thing that you will want to look for in a person is their education. If they have their master's degree and simply love to learn, they might be more to the thinking side than the feeling side. They might also lean toward conscientiousness and being considerate of the feelings and thoughts of other people.

What the person is interested in can help you to speed read them and learn more about their personality as well. If they love to give hugs, for example, they might prefer show love through physical touch. If they are mainly interested in travelling the world with their friends, they might prefer quality time. If they are interested in having alone time or participating in activities that they can do by themselves, they might be introverted or highly sensitive, depending on their other characteristics to determine which one exactly.

Even the tone of a person's voice can tell you more about who they are as a person. If they are quiet and withdrawn, for example, they are probably again either introverted, highly sensitive, or both. If they always have a tone of voice that makes them sound like you are hurting their feelings, they are probably a highly sensitive person. If they speak in a loud, friendly, and almost bubbly way, they are probably extraverted and not at all highly sensitive. If they speak in a way that sounds like they are getting to know your heart, they might be intuitive. If they speak with no emotion and no feelings, they might have less sensitivity than the average person.

When listening to a person talk in an attempt to learn more about who they truly are, it is important to hear more than just the words that the person is saying. You need to hear their tone of voice and pay attention to their body language as well.

For example, when I go out with friends, I often like to pay attention to the body language that I am getting from the other person. Sometimes the conversation flows smoothly, and we can talk all night. Other times, the conversation seems to stall, no matter how many topics I try to bring up.

Now, I could get upset about this or assume the other person is being standoffish here. Or I could take a closer look at my friend, or even a new acquaintance, and see if something else is going on.

Is my friend making eye contact with me or are they avoiding me? Are they smiling or do they seem stressed out? What are their posture, tone of voice, and even the angle of their body able to tell me?

More often than not, I can learn a lot more from those around me by watching those nonverbal cues. Many times, my friends are going to be relieved that someone noticed there was something wrong and was willing to talk it out.

Let's take a look at how studying, rather than reacting, can make a difference. One day I went out with a group of friends and noticed that one of them, let's call him John, seemed like he would rather be anywhere but there. He was frowning, his arms were practically hugging him, and he seemed really annoyed by everyone and everything around him.

The others in the group started to notice that he wasn't conversing and started to poke and prod at him a bit, but they laughed it off and didn't really take it any further. They assumed he was just being a grump and trying to bring down the mood a bit more.

But I knew that there was something else beneath the surface, something that needed to be explored to help him come out of his shell and actually enjoy the night. So, I took John to the side and started to ask a few questions. Before long, John was opening up about his anger with a coworker who had tried to steal the limelight for the work that he, John, had done. This alone was almost enough to get John in trouble at work, and with kids and a wife to support, he was irritated and in no mood to hang out.

Once I understood what the problem was, I was able to take control. We left and headed out for a walk, away from the noise and the nonsense that would just make that kind of mood worse. After a good talk and a few jokes between us to lighten some of the stress, John was able to go home to his wife and kids feeling much more relieved and less stressed out.

Overall, it is clear that there are many factors that go into telling a person's personality. You cannot simply rely on listening to what the person says. You need to look into their appearance, their vocabulary, their occupation, their education level, and what they are interested in. You will need to listen to their words, but at the same time, you will need to watch their body language and their tone of voice to ensure what they are telling you is actually true and that they are not hiding anything.

Let's do another activity to practice what we have learned in this chapter. On the next page, there will be a quiz. Answer the questions to determine what the traits mean in regarding the person's personality. There are no right or wrong answers here, so feel free to think through them and see how they relate to your life.

1. Amanda loves to go to work early and stay late to talk to her coworkers. She speaks loudly and confidently and always has a smile on her face when she's in the midst of conversation. Which personality types does Amanda have and why?

2. Rick is an honest man. He works hard but hates his job. He has many anger outbursts at work, and by the time he gets home, he simply wants to be alone for the rest of the night. Which personality types does Rich have and why?

3. Marshal is the boss of a hard labor shop. He walks around the building four times a day to ensure the production workers are doing their best work. He considers himself as a superior person compared to them. What personality trait does Marshal have and why?

4. Janna is a shy girl. She is happy and does her job well, but she does not like to talk in front of the group at work. When she goes on her lunch break, she eats alone to have a little break from the social interaction.

What personality type does Janna have and why?

Chapter 6: Taking Context Into Account

As we mentioned earlier, sometimes the words that a person says are not what you should be paying attention to, especially while you are speed reading the person who is talking. We talked earlier about how the words that a person speaks might have different meanings based on how exactly they are said and that it is important to listen for more than just words. Now we are going to discuss something called context.

Context is everything that is happening around you while the conversation is going on, the history of the person you are speaking with and any other details that might affect the meaning of the words that are being spoken.

When it comes to speed reading, context is extremely important. For example, if someone is talking about how much they love their work and you notice that their boss is standing right next to them, you might be able to assume that what they are saying could possibly be an exaggeration or it could even be a lie that was said simply to impress their boss. If someone is telling you how much they love their job while no one else is around and you have no involvement with their work whatsoever, you can probably assume that they actually really love their job.

Not only can context change the meaning of what someone is saying but it can also help you read between the lines. In the previous example, I mentioned how someone might be talking about how much they love their work but their boss is standing right next to them, thus casting some doubt on the validity of their claim. Further context in this situation could help you read between the lines of what this person is saying. Let's say, for instance, that this person has told you before that their boss has been really hard on them and is known for reprimanding employees for the smallest infractions. Maybe you also notice that their boss has a scowl on their face and that the employee stiffened as soon as their boss came by. When it is all put together, this context allows you to see a much different message in between the employee's words: I have to say that I love my job because I will get in trouble if I complain about how bad it—or my boss—actually is.

While this might not be the exact message that the employee is trying to convey, context and speed reading of the person who is talking highly suggest that a message like this lies between these lines. You should not make any huge assumptions about what someone is saying beneath their actual words, but a combination of context and your initial reading should give you a good idea of what is actually going on.

Let's look into the things that you should pay attention to while you are looking into the context that a conversation is being had in. The first detail that we will look into is the content of the conversation.

Sometimes the words that a person speaks will have different meanings depending on what has been said throughout the rest of the conversation. For example, if a group of people is talking about how they had hard days at work and another person walks over to talk, they might also say that they had a hard day at work. They really could have had a hard day, but if they seemed otherwise happy until they joined in on this conversation, they might simply be saying this to bond with a group of friends.

Another example would be if someone is talking about the statistics of how many pit bull attacks happen during each year. If they say this during a conversation that is all about loving every type of dog or to a group of pit bull lovers, they might be suggesting that the number is very small. If they say this as the owner of only golden retrievers while they walk past a barking pit bull, they might mean that this number is high and feels scary to them.

As you can see, the content of a conversation can affect the meaning of a person's words.

Action can also affect the meaning of what someone says. If a person is out on a morning run that they partake in every single day and they say that they made some unhealthy choices in their food intake the night before, they probably mean something very different than the person that may say this after spending every evening ordering take-out and watching Netflix in their living room.

Another thing that can affect the context of a conversation is personal habit. If a person has the habit of acting like everything they say is exciting even if it's just a little thing, they might act extremely happy about the fact that they got gas for three cents per gallon cheaper than the day before. If you did not know this person, you might believe that they just get really happy about finding opportunities to save small amounts of money. If you do know this person, then you know that their story is not actually as exciting as it seems because they simply speak enthusiastically about most of the events that happen in their lives.

The next thing that we will talk about that can affect the context of a conversation is a behavioral pattern. For example, if a man tells you that they got into a bar fight the night before, you might be concerned about their safety or even their mental health. You might want to try to help them overcome their struggles. If you know the person well and you know that this type of thing happens just about every weekend, however, your reaction might not come from such a place of shock or sympathy.

The difference between a person telling the truth and a person lying can affect the context of a conversation greatly as well. Of course, if you know that the person whom you are talking to is lying, you know not to believe anything they say. You also know that they have a motive behind the lie and might be able to use your speed-reading techniques to figure out what exactly that motive could be. If you use your speed-reading techniques to tell that a person is telling the truth, however, you will see the context of the conversation and the meaning of its words in a completely different way.

Another thing that can affect the context of a person's words is thought. If a person is thinking about something completely different than the conversation that is being had, their words might be things that they are not thinking about, and they might lack any type of meaning whatsoever. If a person is thinking about what they say carefully, on the other hand, you will know that they truly mean what they are saying and that they care about the topic at hand.

Emotion can also affect the context of a situation. If a person is extremely upset at you or feeling angry, they might say things that they do not mean. If they are in an emotionally stable state of mind, you will be able to better trust what they say.

Even the intention that a person has can affect the context and therefore the meaning of the words that they speak. For example, if they are in a job interview, their intention is to get the job. They might say things that they do not mean or things that might not even be true in order to look impressive to the person who is interviewing them.

Another thing that can affect the context of a conversation is the integrity of the person who is speaking. If you know that they are a person of high integrity, you can probably assume that they are telling the truth. If they are not a person of high integrity, you might want to pay attention to body language that could tell you whether or not they were lying.

Lastly, work habits can affect the context of a conversation. If a person is a hard worker, for example, and they tell you that they had a hard day, you can assume that they probably did. If they like to slack off, you might not want to take them quite as seriously.

Overall, it is easy to see that context can affect a conversation and the meaning of words in big ways. Let's do an exercise so that you can practice your skills relating to context.

In the examples below, come up with ways that context could change the meaning of the words. Be as creative as you would like.

"I worked so hard today. I need to take a break now."

"If you would like to come over for dinner tonight, we would love to have you."

"I love my job. I want to stay at it forever".

"If I didn't live so far away, I am sure that we would hang out way more often."

"Chameleons are difficult pets to keep. Their owners should know more about them before buying them."

"My house is so clean today!"

Chapter 7: Intuition

I have briefly mentioned already that intuition is something that can be used as a tool when you are speed reading the people around you. It is a tool that I personally have used in speed reading very often. In this chapter we will look into what intuition is, learn how exactly to use it in speed reading, and hear a personal story of how strong of a tool intuition truly is.

First, let's look into what intuition really is. Intuition is the feeling that you get about a person or situation even if you don't know much about it. It is the feeling that you can get that makes you feel like you are in danger or makes you feel safe. It is not necessarily a learned skill; it is mostly something that we are born with.

Because of this, intuition can be a strong tool to use in speed reading.

When you use intuition in speed reading, you use it like you do in any other way. Using intuition while reading the people around you is no different than using intuition in the rest of your life.

You will not necessarily have to try to use your intuition. It is something that comes naturally.

Because of this, intuition is not really a tool that you can count on. It is not a tool that you can put in your list of things to use. Sometimes it will come to you while you were reading a person and other times it will not.

The important thing about using intuition while you were reading people is to simply remember to use it when it appears. It is almost like a free tool. It is something you don't have to think about that just happens, and you can use it to your advantage.

There's one particular instance of when my intuition came in handy—and perhaps even saved me—that sticks out in my mind. In my college days, I spent my summers working as a cashier in a small-town garden center. The days were long, and the customers were few and far between, so I spent many hours just caring for the plants and waiting for customers to bring their plants to the checkout aisle.

Because there was not much work to do, I often found myself speed reading the people who came through the store. I would try to discover if they were dads of young kids or busy high-class workers. I would picture what type of garden their personality type would prefer. This helped me to pass the time, and it helped me to better understand my customers. This led to me being able to help the customers in a better way.

One day, however, I did not even have to use my speed-reading techniques. The doors of the garden center opened, and I heard footsteps. My intuition kicked in before I even looked up at the customers that had just entered.

For some reason, my intuition sensed evil in these people. I was able to press the button on my register that told security to come to me before any sort of problem was able to arise. The men walked straight toward me, and the sense of evil grew. Security was in the room before the men even reached the register and when they saw the officers, they turned around and left the store.

In this situation, my intuition was an automatic response. It was my body's way of protecting myself from something that could have turned into a horrible situation. It was fast, and I was not in control of this instinct. I did not even have a chance to think about speed reading these people as my intuition kicked in so fast, but my body's response to the evil that they brought into the store was an instinctual version of speed reading.

Now, this intuition was intense, and typically your experience with this type of speed reading will not be so intense. You might get a feeling that a person could use help with paying for their groceries at the store, for example. You might just get a feeling that someone is not telling the truth when you are talking to them. You might someday even feel intuition as strongly as I did and in an intense situation like I did.

No matter how intuition comes to you, it is important that you listen to it. It is clear that this is one of the strongest speed-reading tools available to you. It is easy to use since you do not need to remember anything; you simply use the feelings as they come. It might be simple to use, but it is still extremely effective. It's a feeling and a speed-reading tool that you never want to ignore.

In addition to saving yourself from potentially harmful situations, as it did for me, your intuition could also help you save the person that you are reading. I have experienced this scenario as well, albeit much more recently while in a session with a client. One of my patients was a mentally disabled war veteran seeing me for PTSD. Despite his PTSD, he was normally a fairly happy, pleasant person. I always had a good feeling when I saw him, and at times, he even made it hard to recognize that he was experiencing trauma beneath all the pleasantries and could be triggered by something as simple as a loud bang.

One day, he came in for his twice-a-week session and something deep in my gut told me something was off. He greeted me the same as always and did not act any differently than normal. Still, my intuition told me that something was very wrong with him. It was not the same feeling of evil that I had that day that those men approached me in the garden center. Instead, this felt more like dread and as though something bad would happen to *him*, not me.

As we carried on with the session, nothing abnormal occurred, but I could not shake that feeling. Finally, I stopped our normal conversation and changed gears to ask my patient if he had had any thoughts of suicide. As always, he told me no, but I kept pressing. My intuition would not stop bugging me about this, so I decided that I would not stop bugging him until I was satisfied that I had the truth. At last, he admitted to me that he had planned on shooting himself as soon as he got home from our session. While I panicked on the inside, I was able to talk him down and convince him to let me take him to the hospital and be put on a psychiatric watch. He was able to get the help that he needed to get him through this hard spot in his life, and I learned for the second time in my life how important my intuition was when it came to speed reading people.

While not a completely reliable tool—my intuition has been wrong before—intuition is also very powerful and useful. You won't always have the luxury of doubting your intuition, especially when it is trying to warn you of an emergency, so get into the practice of following your intuition first and double-checking the reading later. It could just save a life.

For this chapter' exercise, think of a time that you used intuition in your own life and write about it in the space below. This will help you to recognize the feeling of intuition so that you are able to easily recognize it when it is time to use it as a speed-reading tool in the future.

Chapter 8: Asking Questions

Intuition is a strong speed-reading tool, but as we learned in the last chapter, it is not something that you are able to use on command. For a useful tool that you can use whenever you need it, try asking questions. Asking questions is simple and easy to remember because it is natural. It also helps you to learn a lot more about the people you are talking to.

Asking questions can be one of the most useful tools for reading personality and speed reading because it clarifies information that you are not able to understand on your own. Some people might not like to use this tool because it makes it obvious that you are reading or at least trying to get to know the person whom you are talking to. It also requires the reader to actually speak to the person and it cannot be used as a speed-reading tool from across the room.

Even if it requires a little bit more direct work, it is extremely helpful. If you are finding that you do not quite understand a person that you are trying to speed read or you need clarification on something in order to classify the person into a specific personality trait, it can be an extremely helpful, too.

In my occupation, asking questions is key to speed reading patients. At the beginning of the first session I have with a new patient, I only have bare minimal information about who they are and why they have come to me. For example, I might know that a new patient's name is Joanne and that she needs help getting her shopping addiction under control. However, I do not know anything beyond that, such as whether she is introverted or extroverted, if she is more logical or more emotional, if she likes to be in control or prefers to have someone else guide her, and so forth. I will be able to tell some things about Joanne's personality through how she talks, her body language, etc., as we initiate the session. Nevertheless, I will still need ask her some specific questions in order to render a speed reading of her that will help me to help her with her problem.

When you are asking questions, you will want to make sure that you are asking the best possible questions and wording them in the most effective way. For example, if you are trying to figure out how a person feels loved, you might want to ask them if they think a physical gift or an experience is a better birthday present for a child. Their answer might show you if they feel loved best through receiving gifts or quality time. If you simply ask them if they like birthday presents, you probably will not receive a clear and helpful answer.

You will also want to make sure that your questions are on topic. If you ask random questions to the person that you are trying to read, like what they ate for dinner that night, you will not learn much about their personality or who they are as a person. With my hypothetical patient Joanne, for instance, I am going to want to ask her questions that could specifically relate to how her personality might feed into her shopping addiction. A question such as "Do you prefer to go out with friends or stay in on the weekends" could help tell me if she is extroverted or introverted. If she answers with the former, it could mean that she is extroverted and uses shopping as a way to satis-fying her need to be out with others, even if it means breaking the bank. If she answers that she prefers to stay in on the weekends, though, it could point to her being introverted. Her intro-version, then, could indicate that her over-shopping is her special alone time away from family, something that she desperately needs but cannot get at home because her husband and children are always seeking her attention. With the right questions, I will be able to speed read Joanne and get to the source of her problem much more quickly, just like the right questions can help you learn about the personality of whomever you are speaking with.

Another important part of this tool is to not only ask questions but to listen carefully to the an-swers that the people give as well. If you ask a question and do not listen to the full answer, it is almost like you asked the question for nothing. You can do this if you are just conversing with a friend, but if you are really trying to read some-one, you will want the information that you asked for.

When the person is answering your question, you will need to do a few things to make sure that you are listening effectively. You might want to try looking in the eye of the person you are reading. This can help you focus on what they are telling you. You might also want to make mental notes of the information they are giving you.

Lastly, you will want to take the information that they are giving you and relate it to what you are trying to learn. For example, if you are trying to figure out if they are extroverted or introverted, pay close attention to and remember whether they prefer a relaxing night alone or a night out partying with friends.

Overall, we can see that questions are a very helpful tool to use when you are speed reading the people around you. You just need to remember to ask questions that are on topic and that will lead to you learning the information that you need to know. You'll need to actively listen to the answers that the people give as well. If you do these things, asking questions will be able to greatly improve your ability to speed read the people that you are surrounded by.

Asking questions is one of the most under-utilized tools out there. It is easy to feel uncomfortable when we need to start asking questions, and often we shrug it off saying "if they want me to know, they will tell me". Except, most people won't. They don't want to seem like a burden or that they are whining, and so they close themselves up and don't reveal anything.

It is amazing how much we are able to learn from others when we just learn how to turn the focus to them and ask questions. These questions don't have to be in depth and often just following the course of the conversation is going to make it easier.

One time I had a patient named Beth who came into my office to work on her confidence and better understand how she could get over some of her shyness and really get out there and talk to others. This is a common problem that I work with, but what seemed to really get to her was that she didn't like the focus on her, so when someone started asking her questions to open her up, it became easy for Beth to clam up.

While some people like to talk about themselves for hours on end, others like to remain quiet and just listen. So, I suggested to Beth that she just turned the tables. Instead of letting the other person ask her a bunch of questions that she wasn't comfortable with, why didn't she open with questions to the other person?

Within a few weeks, Beth was amazed at how well this was working. Others seemed to just pour out their lives to her and form deep bonds simply because she asked a lot of questions. While you might have to answer a few questions of your own to keep the conversation going, doing this can take the focus from you (if that is something you are worried about) and put the focus back on the other person while helping you to learn so much more about them.

For this chapter's exercise, read the questions below. Then, decide which personality type could be portrayed through the answer. The answers will be on the next page.

1. If you could choose, would you spend a night relaxing at home alone or a night out partying with a group of friends?

2. Would you rather have a massage or go out to dinner with your significant other?

3. Do you like to lead, or do you like to follow?

4. Do you usually make decisions based on facts or based on feelings?

5. Do you typically struggle with anger?

1. Introversion versus extroversion

2. Physical touch versus quality time

3. Dominance versus influence

4. Thinker versus feeler

5. Highly sensitive people versus normal people

Chapter 9: Reliability of Your Readings

Anyone can read the tools in this book and try their hand at speed reading the people around them, but how do you know that your readings are accurate? How accurate are they? How do you know if they are not accurate at all? We will learn all about these questions and how to answer them in this chapter.

First of all, how accurate are our readings? The answer to this question varies not only from person to person but also from conversation to conversation. For example, if you are new to speed reading, your work might not be extremely accurate at first. The more that you learn about personality traits and other tools that you are able to use and the more practice that you get, the more accurate your readings will become. The best speed readers are people who have been reading the people close to them for years. If you practice speed reading for a long time and use the tips that we provide in this book, your results could become extremely accurate.

The accuracy of your speed reading not only depends on how long you have been doing it but also on how much you know. For example, if you just skim over some information on the personality traits and other speed-reading tools, your readings will not be very accurate at all. If you take your time to learn each tool and personality trait and create your own tools that will help you to use this information while you are speed reading people, your readings could again be extremely accurate.

Another thing that affects the reliability and accuracy of your readings is your ability to determine if a person is telling the truth or if they are lying. If you want your readings to be more accurate, you will need to learn the body language signs that show if a person is lying or not.

It is extremely important to have reliable readings because without accurate results, what is the purpose of trying to speed read at all? You are doing this to get to know what a person is like, not to find useless information.

To answer the question of this chapter, yes, speed reading is extremely accurate. In order for it to become accurate, however, the reader needs to be good at what they do. If you want accurate results, you need to know your information, have tools ready to use, and be able to tell whether or not a person is telling the truth. If you can excel at these three things, you can become a speed reader with highly accurate results.

The only way for you to excel at these things, though, is through the same way you master any skill: practice, practice, practice. You need to consciously speed read people whenever the opportunity arises. The best method for practicing speed reading is to just get out there, talk to new people (or people that you hardly know), and see if you can accurately figure out their personalities and how you should interact with them. You will, more likely than not, get your first few readings wrong, at least partially. It's natural. After all, most things are hard to do 100% accurately the first time around. Nevertheless, the more that you try, the better you will get and the more accurate that your speed reading will become.

Chapter 10: When Readings Are Not As They Seem

As you learn to speed read the personalities of the people around you, you will definitely make some mistakes. This is normal, and it is a part of the learning process. How will you know, though, that your results are not correct? When you find out that you have made a mistake, what should you do next? In this chapter, we will discuss the answers to these two very important questions.

First of all, one of the easiest ways to figure out if you have made a mistake is if you have inconsistent results in your readings. For example, if you think that a person is an introvert, but you later learn that they are energized by spending time in groups of friends and by being the center of attention, they are probably not, in fact, considered introverts.

In this situation, you would need to look back at what could have possibly caused your incorrect results. In this particular case, you might have missed that this person is an extrovert but also often wants to work alone or that they seem extremely intuitive. If all of these things are true, they might be both a highly sensitive person as well as an extrovert. The highly sensitive person characteristics might have made it seem like they were introverted, but their extroverted personality was able to show you that you had made a mistake in your reading.

In the circumstance above, the reading was off because the person either did not have enough information when they made their assumption or did not know the categories of the personality traits well enough.

A person might also have an unreliable reading if they are not remembering to take into consideration the context that the conversation was had in. If someone says that they love their job and they often give presentations in front of large groups of people, you might assume that they are extroverted. However, if when looking at the context you realize that the person was not only saying this to you but was saying this to their supervisor as well, it might be either an exaggeration or a lie. This makes the information that they provided you within the conversation unreliable.

Another thing that could make readings unreliable is lies. If a person is lying, their reading is obviously inaccurate and not able to be used. This is why it is important to read the body language of the people that you are speed reading to ensure that they are telling the truth.

Your reading could also be skewed if it is about an emotional topic. If you have high emotions on a topic, you might actually hear what you want to hear from the conversation instead of what is actually being said. Likewise, if you talk about an emotional subject while you are trying to read a person, they might answer in a specific way just so that they can agree with you and avoid unnecessary confrontation. In this situation, you would not be getting an accurate reading of how the person actually felt about the topic. Because of this, it is important that you stay neutral in your conversations if you are trying to speed read the person that you are talking to.

A reading might be off if you do not ask questions or if you do not ask the right questions. It might even be off if you do not listen closely enough to the answers that are provided. If you do not ask questions or if you do not fully listen to the answers, you might be missing information, which would not allow you to get a great and accurate reading.

Readings might also be affected if you as the reader use a snap judgement. Snap judgements are made quickly and without a lot of background information. They typically should not be used in speed reading at all. If you are using them, it should only be on topics that have distinctive answers and if you are well versed in speed reading to the point that you are able to run through all of the different categorizations and tools in your mind in an extremely quick manner. It's basically a tool that should be avoided unless you are a speed-reading expert with years of experience.

So, let's look at a list of things that can make your readings unreliable or inaccurate:

- Lack of knowledge on speed reading techniques or personality categorizations

- Making assumptions

- Not asking questions

- Asking the wrong questions

- Not listening to the answers that are given to you

- The use of snap judgement when not yet an expert at speed reading with years of experience

For this chapter's exercise, remember a time in your life that you thought something about a person you were talking to but ended up being completely wrong. What caused your incorrect judgement? How is this similar to incorrect readings that you will come across as you start to practice your new skill of speed reading? This will help you to see how speed reading can have accurate results. You will be able to think back on this exercise once you begin speed reading to help you make fewer mistakes than you otherwise would.

In the next chapter, we are going to learn how to interact with people of different personality types. And if you like what you've learned so far, or you've found benefit, feel free to leave a review on Amazon. I really appreciate it as your feedback means a lot to me.

Chapter 11: How To Interact with People of Different Personality Types

Why do you want to learn how to speed read the people around you? Speed reading has many great benefits, but one of the best is that it allows you to interact well with the people around you. You can interact with people based on how their specific personality traits respond. In this chapter, we will look at the best ways to interact with each separate personality type.

First, let's look into how to interact with people based on their personality types. If a person is an extrovert, they will love to talk to you, for example. Extroverts might respond well if you ask them questions because they are able to talk about themselves while they answer. Introverts, on the other hand, might do best in a calm and quiet conversation between just the two of you.

A person with intuition might want to hear about your personal situations before they share their own. A sensing person might open up if you start a conversation based on facts about the past instead of future ideas.

A thinker might want to tell you more about who they are if you give them a chance to talk about justice. A feeler might want to talk about the things that they love in the world or the people that they are close to.

If you are talking to a judging person, you might need to make sure that you are talking about things that they agree with. A perceiver might be more open-minded and able to talk about a wider variety of viewpoints and topics.

If you are talking to a person with the dominance trait, it is important to know that they talk in a direct fashion. You might want to avoid off-topic statements and jokes with these people as they are mainly focused on the purpose of the conversation. It is also important to note that they are very driven, so they might open up to you if you talk to them about their goals in their life or their career field.

A person with the influence trait should be talked to in a very different manner. They are imaginative, so they might enjoy discussions about creative and new ideas. They might relate well to you if you discuss abstract things with them.

People with the steadiness trait are described as being sweet. They might like to talk about your personal life or about things that they are passionate about. Ask questions to these people and see what they bring up. It will probably be their passion, and it will be a good place to start your conversation with them.

Conscientious people might be the most difficult to get to know well. They are known for being cautious, which might make it hard for them to relate to new people. It is important that you keep this in mind while you talk to them. You might want to talk to them about their current project or their work as they are described as being competent, so this might help them open up to you a little bit more than they otherwise would.

Next, we will look into how you should interact with a person based on if they are highly sensitive or normal. With a highly sensitive person, it is important that you remember that their emotions and reactions run hot. If you know this well before beginning a conversation with them, you might be able to avoid emotional topics altogether. You will need to remember that highly sensitive people are easily offended and easily irritated so that you can be careful with your words as you converse with them. It is also important to note that highly sensitive people prefer to work alone, so if they seem to be getting upset or overwhelmed, you might want to end the conversation early and give them some space to relax and recharge. With normal people, these things should not matter in your conversations.

Even how people give and receive love can be used to help you to interact better with those around you. For example, if you are talking with a person who tends toward words of affirmation, you might want to compliment them as they talk about their work.

If you are talking with someone who prefers acts of service, consider opening the door for them while walking into the building to allow them to accept you more. You could also consider helping them with some tasks when they are busy to get to know them better in a way that they would respond extremely well to.

If you are talking with a person who feels most loved when receiving gifts, consider bringing them a coffee to the early morning meeting that you are having. You could even just bring them some resources that you think would help them in their work. If they receive anything from you, they will respond better to your conversation.

If a person reacts best to physical touch, make sure to shake their hand when you meet them and anytime you start a conversation with them. Consider reaching out a hand and touching their shoulder quickly when they say something meaningful if it is appropriate in the specific situation. These things will help your interaction with the person because they will feel welcomed and acknowledged.

Lastly, if they prefer quality time, consider spending some time with them outside of work. Invite them out for drinks at the end of the day or for lunch on the weekend. As they spend more time with you, they will open up more to speaking with you.

As you can see, every single personality trait can teach us how to interact with the person who holds it. Whether it's something as noticeable as introversion or extroversion or something as small as how they receive love, these things can help us greatly in both our goals of speed reading and our ability to interact with the people around us.

For this chapter's exercise, take the personality types below. Pretend that you know that your new work partner has this personality trait. How will you use this knowledge to both get to know and work well with this person?

1. Extroversion

2. Physical Touch

3. The Trait of Being Conscientious

4. Highly Sensitive Person

Chapter 12: How To Speak the Language of Other Personality Types

Sometimes when you are speed reading people, it will be not enough to simply know what their personality types are. Sometimes you will actually need to speak their language. In this chapter, we will look into how you can speak the language of different personality types.

First, let's look into what this really means. By "speak in the language of a different personality type", I mean talking and acting in a way that the other person will appreciate and understand. This means that you should have the ability to not only know what a person's personality type is but also how to act like you have the same one in order to get to know them better or in order to read them better.

Basically, the way that you will get to know a person is by speed reading the room and the way that you will speak their language is by acting like you have the same personality traits. Now, I know that you do not actually have these traits. I also know that you probably do not want to lie about who you are. You do not need to do either of these things. You simply need to act in a way that you know they will enjoy because of their personality type.

Let's consider that you are an introvert talking to an extrovert. If you want to get to know them better or if you want to allow them to like you, you will need to speak their language. It is OK that you are an introvert, but you will need to act a little bit extroverted in this conversation. For example, you might want to have a conversation in a public place around many other people.

This is because, as we already know, this is the comfort place for an extrovert where they rest and recharge. You might want to take other things that you know about extroverts and involve them in the conversation as well. For example, we know that extroverts like to be the center of attention. Since you know this, you might want to make the conversation about the extrovert and not about you. This will give them the type of conversation that they feel the best in so that they are able to share more about themselves. With these tips, you will be able to get the extrovert talking, and you will be able to get to know them better. You will also probably be able to make them like you better.

My sister has given me much insight into how introverts can speak with extroverts. As a lawyer, she has no choice but to interact with a wide variety of people in both her professional and personal lives. She explained to me that there have been many times when she has gone out and talked to someone who would be considered an extrovert. She admitted that these individuals can be a lot of fun, and as an extrovert, I have to agree. They like to socialize, start up a conversation, and seem at ease with almost anyone in the room. My sister, on the other hand, is very much an introvert and usually prefers to stick with a few close friends whenever possible.

Does this mean that she ran off as soon as she could to avoid situations involving strangers who are extroverts? Of course not. Some of her best friends are extroverts, and this is a good chance to meet someone new! Still, she had to come in and make some changes to her own style of talking, to learn how they could bounce ideas off of each other and help them to really get the rapport going.

Extroverts like to be social. So, my sister had to make herself social. Did this mean that she lied to them about who she was? Of course not! She does like to meet new people, and it's not like she is scared of talking. She is just not typically the kind of person to be the first to approach anyone. So, she decided to bring the joy she gets from meeting new people and her ability to carry on a conversation out front and center and use them to her advantage to get along with the extroverts that she comes into contact with, whether it is for work or when she is out with her pre-existing friends. And you know what? More often than not, it works out great!

Let's look at another example. Imagine that you were talking to a person who is labeled as a highly sensitive person according to your speed-reading test. You know that this person is easily irritated and easily offended. Because you know these things, you will want to avoid any type of controversial act or conversation. You will also want to avoid anything that you know they do not like.

In my experience, these kinds of people are few and far between. Still, you have to be more selective with the topics that you choose with them. For example, choosing to talk about the weather or asking how they know the host of the party can be safe topics to get the ball rolling.

I have also found that letting them take the reins and rule the conversation can help. These individuals will stick with topics they are familiar with, and you can follow their lead. Try not to offer up a new topic with this individual and you are sure to keep things going smoothly.

For example, you will not want to stay and talk to them when they are trying to have their alone time because you know that they love their alone time and this might irritate them. You also might want to talk about emotional things with them because they will be able to relate. It might not be the most fun conversation for you, but for them, it will be a bonding experience. It will also give them the chance to share more about themselves, which will, in turn, give you the chance to get to know them better.

Lastly, let's consider a conversation between you and a person who is intuitive. An intuitive person might read you and know exactly how you are feeling and thinking. As a speed reader, you will be using your intuition as well. You might want to let the intuitive person read into who you truly are so that they allow you to do the same for them.

Overall, speaking the personality language of another person is very simple. You need to take what you know about that personality and use it in your conversation. It is a simple tip but very effective. Speaking the language of the people around you according to their personality types helps you to read them better and get to know them better. It allows them to feel more comfortable, so they open up more to you. It will help you greatly in your speed-reading journey.

Chapter 13: How To Date Or Become Friends with People of Different Personality Types

As you know, people are all different, and many of the people that you love and feel close to might have different personality types than you do. Because of this, in order to make new friends and keep those friends that you have today, you will need to know how to interact with people of different personality types.

For example, a friendship might seem difficult at first if one friend is an introvert and the other is an extrovert. The two people might have a hard time relating to each other even if they have many other things in common. They might struggle to find things that they both enjoy doing together.

In order to avoid situations like this, you will need to know how to be friends with people of all personality types. You can begin this process by speed reading the people you make friends with to figure out what type of personality traits they have. Then, you can use the tips that we will go over in the rest of this chapter to create lasting friendships despite any differences you might have.

If you are friends with an introvert, you will need to understand that they need time and space to be alone sometimes. This is not any type of offense to you or anything you did, but it is because their alone time is the way that they recharge themselves. If you are friends with an extrovert, you will need to know that it is OK for you to turn down some of their request to spend time with you. If you are overwhelmed by how much they want to do with you, do not feel bad. It is simply because they love spending time out with friends.

If you are friends with an intuitive person, be ready for them to talk to you about their future often. You might even want to bring up their future because it will make them feel appreciated and heard. If you are friends with a sensor, you might want to talk about more practical or present and past relating things.

If you are friends with a thinker, you might want to talk about facts and evidence when you are trying to prove a point. If you are friends with a feeler, however, you will want to talk about emotions and how you feel about things when you were trying to make a point. These tips will help you to relate to your friend and help them to understand how you are feeling better.

If you are friends with a perceiver, you might get many requests to do spontaneous activities. It is OK if you do them and it is OK if you turn them down. Just make sure that your friend knows that you are still close to them even if you do not like spontaneous things. Perceivers love spontaneous things, so you might need to voice this clearly. If you are friends with a judger, on the other hand, things might be more planned and precise.

Next, let us look into being friends with a highly sensitive person. If you were friends with a highly sensitive person, you need to know that what they do is not bad. Their emotions are not always negative, and there is nothing wrong with the way that they act. Highly sensitive people are simply people who feel things more than others. This can even be a good thing. It is important to remember as the friend of a highly sensitive person that they are easily offended and easily irritated. You will not want to say things that could hurt their feelings, and you will not want to continue to bother them after they have already turned you down on something. You will also need to remember that their emotions seem bigger than they are. If your friend gets mad at you and yells at you, give them a chance to calm down. Things will probably be OK in a few minutes.

If you are friends with a person who is not highly sensitive, you won't need to worry about these things. They will probably not be easily offended or easily irritated. They will probably have a normal emotional reaction. This is not to say that you should still not be careful to not hurt their feelings because this is important in any relationship with any type of person. You simply want to treat your friends well.

So, what if you want to be friends with someone who is a very different personality type than you are? What if you are different in not just one personality trait but in most—or all—of them? Considering how you have to adjust your approach so much for each different personality type or trait, you might think that it's too much work to be friends with someone with a very different personality from your own—perhaps even a personality that is the exact opposite of yours. However, it is not impossible. I know from firsthand experience.

As I showed in chapter four, my sister and I have very different personality types in many ways. She is an introvert, a thinker, and a judger as well as dominant and conscientious. I, however, am an extrovert, a feeler, and a perceiver with influence and steadiness traits. All that we really have in common when it comes to our personality types is that we are both sensors and normal types rather than highly sensitive. Regardless, we manage to not only get along but be close friends. It just takes each of us being willing to accommodate some of the other's personality traits.

For example, when I want to spend time with my sister, I let her decide where we are going to be and what we are going to do. This helps her as an introvert because she gets to be in a setting with fewer people and as a dominant as she is able to have choices and control over the situation. Similarly, she tries to tap into her more emotional side in order to work with my feeler traits and to allow us to connect on the feelings that I thrive on. She also makes sure to let me know that she appreciates when I do something nice for her and to congratulate me on my accomplishments, even the small ones, to appeal to my influencer side.

Most importantly, we have talked and agreed on certain things we will not do or discuss to prevent our differing personalities from clashing. A key topic we avoid is politics. With her being more of a judger and me more of a feeler, we cannot seem to approach politics in the same manner, even if we come to the same conclusions, and that often causes heated clashes if we ever drift into that territory. Just by avoiding where we cannot work with each other's personalities, we save ourselves from a lot of awkward or painful interactions.

It's important that when you are friends with someone as different from your personality type(s) as my sister and I are, you work together to accommodate your differences. By speed reading their personality type(s) from the first moment you meet them, you will be able to start on this negotiation right away, and you might just make the best friend you will ever have.

Now, let's look into how to be friends with someone based on how they receive love. If your friends prefer words of affirmation, you might want to tell them how great of a friend they are often. If you do not tell them this, they might not feel your friendship as deeply. This is because they react well to words and they feel loved when they hear good things about themselves.

If you are friends with someone who feels love through receiving gifts, you might want to bring them little things every once in a while. It is probably a good idea to not forget this friend's birthday and to give them a nice gift on this day. It is not because your friend is spoiled or needs material things; often, it is simply how they feel love.

If your friend is most receptive to quality time, you will want to make sure that you say yes when they invite you to do things. You will also want to make sure to invite them to do things every once in a while. They will grow closer to you as a friend during the time that you spent together because it is what they really appreciate it and look forward to. It is what makes them feel loved.

If you are friends with a person who best receives love through physical touch, you might want to give them a hug when you see them. If they do something awesome, you might want to give them a high-five. They will feel more connected to you as a friend the more they touch you.

Lastly, if you are friends with someone who feels most loved when receiving acts of service, you will want to do little things for them whenever you could. If you have a chance to help them out with a difficult task that they have to do at home, they will really appreciate it. If you are meeting them for lunch, consider paying for the meal for them or giving them a ride home afterward so they don't have to walk. All of these things will help your friend to feel loved.

How Different Personalities Express Love

I remember a time when my partner and I were just not getting along. I felt like I was doing everything in my power to help make the relationship work. I found that my way to show love and affection was all about gifts, and so I tried to shower them with gifts, but this meant I had to work more and was gone from home.

The problem was that gifts were not the way my partner showed love. Quality time was how they felt loved. They were upset because we hardly had time to spend together as I had to work to pay for the gifts. Once this misunderstanding was cleared up, the pressure was lifted from both of us. I got to relax more and work less, and my partner of the time got to spend more time with me as well!

Hopefully, after this chapter, you will be able to get along with people and become friends with people who have different personality types than you do. The most important thing is to simply understand the personality types and use the things that they like to your advantage. This trick not only works with friendships; it also works with romantic relationships. Next, we will look into how to use personality types to better your romantic relationships with the people that you are dating.

If you are dating someone who is an extrovert, you might want to take them out on dates in public places often. They will appreciate the interaction with the people that you see. You are dating an introvert. However, you might want to have most of your dates at home where they feel the most comfortable.

If you are dating a thinker, you might want to talk about serious subjects and academic things with them. If you are dating a feeler, you might want to talk about love and emotions with them. These are just things that help them to feel close and related to you.

If you are dating someone who is an intuitive, you might want to talk about what you would like your future to be with them. If you are dating a sensing person, you will want to talk about practical things that you are dealing with and present time.

If you are dating someone who is a perceiving person, you might want to make last-minute plans and participate in their spontaneous activities. If you are dating a judging person, however, you will want to keep things much better planned.

If you are dating a highly sensitive person, it is similar to being friends with a highly sensitive person. It is important to simply remember that their feelings are valid and their reactions are typical of the type of personality that they have. There's nothing wrong with being a highly sensitive person. You will never want to judge a highly sensitive person for the reactions that they have. If you are careful around your partner, you will be able to support them with their large emotions. Remember that their large emotions give them large hearts and that they are able to share even more love with the people around them than normal people are. You might even want to consider yourself lucky to be with a highly sensitive person in a romantic relationship.

I know this from personal experience—my partner is a highly sensitive person. They can be overly emotional and, as the personality type suggests, sensitive. While they express their love through spending quality time with me, they really prefer to work and be alone outside of that time together, and God help you if you do not give them that time to themselves. However, they are also the kindest person I have ever known. They are very loving and passionate as well as intuitive. Every feeling they have is felt unbelievably deeply, including their love for me, and I am grateful for that every day.

Do not get me wrong, it can, at times, be a struggle to be in a romantic relationship with a highly sensitive person. My partner often gets emotional for things that I find to be no big deal. For example, one time I had to arrive home late on date night because paperwork at my office had taken longer than I had originally anticipated. I was still able to make it home in time for us to make it to a late movie and have Polish dogs in the theater. Nevertheless, my partner still got very upset and would hardly speak to me the rest of the night. I made the mistake of telling them that I thought that they were overreacting since I had called to tell them ahead of time and we were still able to spend the night together. They got even more up-set, and as soon as we got home, my partner wanted nothing more than to be left alone. The next day, they still were not talking to me. I finally apologized for what I had said and reminded them—and myself—that their feelings were valid and that their reaction was just how they handle disappointment. They cooled down, told me that they realized it was no big deal, but also thanked me for acknowledging that their feelings were not ridiculous for them. We were then able to spend the quality time that we both wanted together the rest of the day, and everything turned out fine.

It is also important that you know how the person you are dating likes to receive affection so that you are able to make them feel loved because feel-ing loved is simply the point of a relationship. If you are not able to make your partner feel loved, your relationship will probably not work out. This makes how a person receives love a strong tool to use in romantic relationships.

To use these love categories in your relationship, first figure out which category your partner falls under. Then figure out the category that you tend to use most often without thinking about it. If these two categories are different, make it a point to use the love category of your partner. It will make a huge difference in your relationship guaranteed.

Overall, it is easy to see that having relationships, both romantic and friendships, is something possible but a little bit tricky to do with people of different personality types. If you are going to have any type of relationship with someone who has a different personality type than you do, you will need to learn about their personality. You can start this by speed reading the person to figure out what types of traits they carry. You will then want to do things that that type of personality enjoys and appreciates. If you get to know the personality of the person that you are friends with or the person that you were dating, the relationship between you will be stronger than ever.

For this chapter's exercise, pick any friend that you are close to in life right now. Think of the person they portray themselves as and speed read them based on this. There are going to be a few different personality types that you are able to work with based on which part of their personality you would like to focus on and which one seems to explain them the best. Many times, exploring a few different tests will make a difference in determining who they really are.

Chapter 14: Speed Reading People in A Workplace

So far, we have talked in detail about what speed reading is as well as the things that you need to know in order to do it. We have talked about personality versus character as well as the different personality categorization tools that can be helpful to use while you are speed reading people. We also started to learn how to interact with people of specific personality types. In the next large segment of this book, we are going to discuss how to use speed reading well in different situations.

First, let's look into the workplace. When you go to work, you have to deal with people every single day. In some jobs, you might deal only with your direct coworkers whom you share an office space with while in other jobs you might interact with hundreds of customers in a short amount of time. Some jobs might even involve you speaking in front of thousands of people at a time. No job, however, is alone. Even if you work online from the comfort of your home, you are either conversing with or doing work for at least one other person. Clearly, every working person deals with other people to some extent throughout their workday. Because of this, speed reading must be a helpful tool to use in the workplace.

First, let's look into how to network with people while using speed reading. If you are trying to do business with someone by networking with them, it will definitely help if you stand out to them. You can make yourself stand out by understanding who they are as a person as well as by interacting with them in a way that makes them feel good about themselves.

For example, if a person is an introvert, you might want to create a comfortable and quiet setting for your meetings that is away from large groups of people. You might even want to do a large amount of the communication to them via email so that they are able to have more alone time to rest and recharge.

Next, let's look at how to act and react with our coworkers according to our speed-reading results. How you act with your coworkers based on the who they are according to your speed-reading results is the same as you should act with any person that has their same personality traits and characteristics.

Let's say a person is a highly sensitive person, for example. You should act with them in a way that will not offend them or irritate them, as highly sensitive people are both easily offended and easily irritated. You also may want to talk with them via email so that they feel more like they are able to work alone and have their own space.

You can also use your speed-reading knowledge to help you learn how to persuade people in the workplace. This can be extremely helpful for salespeople. If a salesperson is trying to sell their product, they will have a much easier time by knowing their audience well. If the seller knows the personality traits that their buyer has, they will be able to make a significantly larger number of sales with the same amount of effort that they were using before.

You can even use speed reading techniques to sell yourself in the workplace. If you are trying to impress a boss or a coworker, you can look into who they are as a person to see what they would be the most impressed by. If they are a dominant person, you would want to directly tell them what your goal is and what you need from them. If they are a feeler, however, you may want to bring up new ideas about the future in abstract ways to impress your boss with your creativity.

Lastly, we will look into how to use speed reading in a workplace when you are the main boss. You can use your speed-reading techniques to read your employees in order to know them better and to see their unique and specific skills. This way of finding a worker's unique and specific skills is perhaps best used when you need to train new managers. People who are in charge of others at work need to know and understand the people that work for them. You could teach your new managers to use speed-reading techniques in order to get to know their employees and in order to see their capabilities, just like you do in your own job.

Overall, we can definitely see that speed reading is a valuable tool in the workplace. We have mentioned only a few examples and tools to use in the workplace, though we know that there are many more ways to use speed reading at work as well.

For this chapter's activity, come up with three new ways to use speed reading at work. Try using your own specific workplace. For an added challenge, consider actually using your ideas in real life when you are at work over the course of the next week. See if it can change your experience and success rate while dealing with other people at your job.

Chapter 15: Speed Reading Potential Employers

When you are in the process of looking for and applying for a new job, things can feel scary. Even if you are not completely happy at your current job, you at least know what things are like. You know who your boss is and how he treats you. The same is usually not true when you are interviewing for a job with a different company in a new location. Thankfully, speed reading can help with this uncomfortable situation.

When you interview for a new job, you can speed read the person who is interviewing you. When you do this, you will be able to learn much more about how your future job would be if you chose to work for this person.

The personality types that they interviewer has can help you to understand what it would be like to work for them in the future and to see them on what would probably be a daily basis. For example, if the interviewer seemed to have the telltale signs of an overly sensitive person, you might want to be careful around them. If you offended them or irritated them during the interview, for example, you would probably not get the job. You would also have to decide if working for an overly sensitive person would be something that you could do or would want to do every day of your life.

Other personality traits like introversion and extroversion can affect the experience that you have with your boss as well. If you are looking for a job where your duties are communicated clearly and feedback is given often and at an honest rating, you might want to work for an extrovert. If you would rather not have conversations with your boss unless you have to, you might feel better about working for an introvert.

You might want to consider how good of a leader the interviewer is as well if you are looking for a role model who is able to help you gain momentum in your field. If you want a good example and someone who can lead you well while you are at work, you might want to work for someone who has the influence trait.

These qualities can all make great leaders and great bosses, but what else should you look for in the person interviewing you so that you are able to have a happy and successful work environment? You could consider looking for traits in the person that are similar to yours. For example, if you both receive and give love the same way, you might work well together and be able to show appreciation for each other's work in a stronger way than anyone of different love categories ever could.

If you are currently at a job where you love your boss, you might want to look for a job where the person who is interviewing you has many personality similarities to the person that you already work for. This could help you to ensure that you would feel happy and welcome at the new job and that it would simply be a good fit for you.

Speed reading during an interview is not only to see if you would like to boss and do well at the job, however. Speed reading can also be used in an interview to negotiate. We all know that sometimes, to get what you need or want from a new job, you need to negotiate. Whether you need to make a slightly higher wage than the one that they are offering or you need a few more vacation days per year, it is important to know how to negotiate before you go into the interview.

With speed reading, this negotiating process can be easy. The first thing you should do is make sure that the interviewer has a good impression of you. You can use their personality traits that you are able to read in order to make sure that they can relate to you and that they like you.

For example, if the person who is interviewing you seems to be a thinker and not a feeler, you might want to keep your conversation based on past and present events. You might want to mention more facts than abstract ideas. With this way of talking, the interviewer will better relate to you and will most likely like the person that you are. If they like who you are, they are much more likely to give you the things you want and need while you are in the midst of negotiating with them.

Speed reading can also be helpful in interviews when difficult conversations arise. Interview conversations are never easy, but they get even more difficult when controversial topics are brought up and when hard to answer questions are asked.

However, these things are common in interviews because they help the employer get to know who the interviewee truly is.

For example, if you are asked about your stance on politics in your interview, you might want to read the person who asked the question before you answer. Of course, you always want to be honest in an interview, but it might help if you word your answer carefully in a way that you believe the interviewer would either agree with or at least understand and accept.

Overall, it is easy to see that speed reading can help the interview process in huge ways. It can help you to know what kind of boss you are talking to so that you know if you would like to work with them and if you would work well together. It helps you to negotiate, and it helps you to have success even in the most difficult of conversations. Next time you have an interview, be sure to use speed reading to help it go as well as possible.

Preparing for Your Interview Exercise

Preparing for an interview at a new job is one of the best ways to calm your nerves and help you bring the confidence that is needed to be successful. To help you prepare, answer the questions below to determine how well the interview is going and to see if there are some ways that you can improve an interview that might not be going exactly how you want.

What signs would you look for to determine the interview is going well when reading the interviewer across the desk?

Are there any signs that would make you feel like you would not get the job, and how can you use speed reading to turn things around?

What red flags might come up that tell you, this job isn't for me?

Chapter 16: Speed Reading In-terviewees

In the last chapter, I talked about how speed reading can benefit you while you are trying to get a new job, but did you know that it can also be a huge help from the other side? Speed reading can actually help interviewers get to know the people who are applying for their job opening. It can help you get to know them on a more personal level than asking and answering questions can provide. It can tell you what type of worker they would be, and it can help you to decide whether or not they would be a good fit for your company.

First, let's look into how speed reading can help you get to know the interviewees on a more individual and personal level. When you interview a person, you typically only get to know them based on how they answer questions. What if, though, the person whom you are interviewing is an introvert and is feeling too uncomfortable to give great answers? This does not take away their chance at being the perfect fit for the job in most cases, excluding jobs where social interaction is key, but it does take away your ability as the interviewer to get to know them well through the questions that you ask.

If the person who you are interviewing is an introvert, you will be able to tell from the personality signs and traits while you are reading them. You might notice that they seem quiet or that they mention activities that they can do alone. If you see these characteristics and that the person is uncomfortable in the interview, you might need to take a different approach to getting to know them better.

You might want to consider talking to them softly and calmly. You could move the interview to a more private place if you were previously talking in a crowded, public space. You could try to give questions that are either easy to answer or that you know the person is very interested in. All of these tips and tricks might help the interviewee to feel more comfortable and able to share their real talents and skills with you in an open and honest way.

After you get the interviewee to open up about who they really are and what they are capable of, you can begin to use speed reading to tell what type of worker they would be. Do they have the dominance trait? If so, they will probably be dedicated to their job and determined to become successful in what they do. Are they extroverted and easily distracted? If so, you might find them chatting with friends every time you leave the room.

You might even want to use speed reading to see how well a person knows themselves. If your readings do not add up to what they are honestly telling you, they might not know much about how to properly implement their own skills and their own personality.

It is up to you to decide whether you think their personality type and traits would allow them to be a good worker or a poor one. Of course, every type of personality trait that people have can add to them doing great at a specific job if they use their skills wisely. You just need to ensure that your company truly is the best fit for them and the best way for their unique talents and abilities to be put to good use.

For one last note, it might also be smart to look for signs of lying when you are interviewing someone and using speed reading. If you discover body language that shows the person is lying, they might not be a good fit for your job opening. You would really not be able to tell well because you would not know what they said that was the truth and what they said that was a lie.

Speed reading can also help you to be able to tell if the person that you are interviewing would be a good fit for your company. Consider the employees that you already have. Would this new person be able to get along with the workers that already work for you every day? Would they be able to be motivated by each other or would they distract each other? Would the workplace be bettered by this new person's presence or would additional drama be brought in with them? Knowing if a person will fit within your company is an important thing to figure out, and with speed reading, it can be quick and easy.

You might be hesitant to hire—or not hire—someone based on your speed reading of them during the interview. After all, the interviewee could have just been too nervous to show who they really are as a person. They might come across as too shy and introverted during an interview because they despise interviews but be a great worker and outgoing person under normal circumstances. This is when context will be one of your closest allies in rendering accurate readings. Nevertheless, speed reading during the interview will give you an idea of what this person is like, and when you take every aspect of your reading together, context included, you should have a good enough image of this person to decide whether or not to hire them.

Do not just ignore your speed reading of an interviewee because you assume that they were nervous about the interview.

One time, I needed a new secretary at my office after my former secretary had to move to another state for his partner's job. My previous secretary had been such a great fit with my patients and me that I knew it would be difficult to replace him. However, I needed a new secretary quickly, which made me a little sloppy when it came to the interviewing process. One interviewee had stood out due to her experience and recommendations, but things did not quite click in the interview. After observing the way she talked and fidgeted during the interview, I came to the conclusion that she was a bit too extroverted, someone who could potentially be easily distracted by conversation. She also seemed to have a judgmental tone when talking about clients at her previous job, which had been at a psychiatrist's office. My intuition also kept raising the red flag at me, like it just knew that there was something about her that would rub me the wrong way. Still, her resumé was the best I had seen so far and I really needed a new secretary to take over before all the calls and appointments got out of hand, so I brushed it off to her being nervous about the interview and hired her anyway.

This decision turned out to be one of my worst. My initial speed reading of this woman had been correct. I often caught her talking on the phone with people who were not patients, she would get sidetracked with online chat, and her attitude toward my patients was horrible. I soon found out that she was gossiping about some of my patients on her Facebook page and fired her immediately. If I had just trusted my speed reading during the interview, I could have saved myself from this headache and prevented the almost destruction of my practice.

We can clearly see that speed reading can be helpful when you are interviewing a person to work for an open position that you have available. You can use it to ask the right questions, to see if they would be a good fit for your company, and to see if they would get along with and work well with the employees that you already have. You can even use speed reading to make an interview more comfortable or to see if a person is lying when they answer your questions. Speed reading can benefit the interview process in many ways. It is a tool that should be used in interviews by interviewers and interviewees alike whenever possible because it simply provides so many benefits.

Chapter 17: Speed Reading for Teachers

If you think about speed reading and all its benefits, it is easy to see why speed reading would be beneficial for teachers. It would allow them to know their students better. It would let them see into how they can better reach their students at each of their own individual levels. It would even allow teachers to better understand how each of their students learns on an individual level.

This is not the only way that speed reading can help teachers, however. These tools can actually help teachers before they even get a job and while they are in the midst of their teacher training.

College professors and other teacher trainers can use speed-reading techniques to ensure that they are producing the best teachers possible.

The trainer can speed read the future teachers as well. The trainer can decipher which personality categories the future teacher fits into. They can then help them grow as a teacher based on these traits. This would allow the trainees to grow into the best teachers that they can possibly be.

For example, the trainer can see if a teacher feels loved through receiving gifts or through quality time. The trainer can then get to know the teacher and show appreciation for them in this way. If the trainer does this, the teacher might remember it and pass it on to her own class. If she feels and gives love through receiving gifts, she might pass out stickers to the little children in her classroom after they have an exceptional day. If she prefers quality time, she might create an extended recess with class activities where she can play games with her students to get to know them on a more individual and personal level.

The trainer could even consider teaching the future teachers about speed reading. If the future teachers knew about speed reading, they would be able to use it in their own classrooms. It would allow the teachers to know each student and their learning style individually so that the students could have the best possible success rate.

These teachers and trainers might even be able to change speed reading to fit their own needs. For example, they could change the personality categorization tool list to include something along the lines of learning styles.

According to learning styles online, there are seven different types of learning styles. These types include visual, logical, verbal, physical, aural, social, and solitary. Visual learners learn by seeing the information or by seeing something happen. Logical learners learn by considering what exactly makes sense in the specific situation. Verbal learners prefer to speak while they discover new things, and physical learners prefer to explore with their sense of touch. Aural learners will learn best by listening to the information that they need to know. Social learners prefer to gain knowledge with a group of friends while solitary learners do their best work when they are alone.

A teacher would be able to tell which learning style each student has by simply observing them. If the teacher notices one child is constantly running their fingers over the scientific models in the classroom and always has the top grade when it's a lab project day, that child is probably a physical learner. If a child has a hard time in class discussions but does great on every test, they might be a solitary learner. If a young boy remembers every single word of all the lectures from the week before and quotes your exact words when discussing the topics with his friends, he might be an aural learner. If a girl stands while she reads and paces while she thinks, she might be a physical learner.

If a teacher memorized these and added them to the speed-reading profile, she would be able to quickly notice how each child in her class prefers to learn. This would allow her to teach each child individually in the best way possible.

It would be important for the teacher to know that students typically have two of these seven learning styles. They usually have one of the styles that include visual, logical, verbal, physical, and aural that allows them to learn to their best capability. They will also learn best through either social or solitary settings.

Trainers of teachers could use this strategy in the same way. They could look into the learning styles of each of the future teachers so that they can train them in the most beneficial way to each individual that they were in charge of.

Overall, we can tell that speed reading is a tool that is extremely beneficial when it is used in the education system. First, it can be used by trainers who train teachers so that they are able to make the best teachers in history by getting to know them on an individual and personal level. It can also be used by classroom teachers in the same way. Perhaps in the most unique form, speed reading can be used in education to help teachers and trainers to learn the learning styles of their students. Overall, speed reading is a tool that can greatly benefit teachers and trainers of teachers alike when it used in the field of education.

For this chapter's exercise, think about what learning style you do best with. Why do you do best with this learning tool? What outward signs do you portray that could possibly show others what your specific learning style is?

Chapter 18: Personality Types in Children

Reading the personalities of children and kids seems difficult because children do not necessarily know who they are entirely before they are grown up. Their personalities are still changing on a daily basis as they get to know themselves. Regardless of these two things, it is possible to get to know the personality types of the children in your life. In this chapter, we will learn how to do just that.

First, let's talk about how children do not necessarily know who they are when they are young.

Young children might not even be aware of their personality or what a personality really is. They might not be able to tell you if they are introverted or extroverted because they don't even know what those words mean. Because of this, you will have to rely completely on readings and not necessarily on what they tell you because they are not able to tell you very much concrete information.

Even younger children might not be able to talk. If you are trying to read the personality of a child who cannot talk, you will have to look only at their actions. This is OK, though, because you can still tell how their first personality type is forming and be able to speed read them based on this.

Next, let's look into the fact that children are still changing on a daily basis. Young people are still trying to determine who they are and who they want to be in this world. They also do not have much life experience, so they have not gone to the events that will shape who they are going to be as grown-ups. This makes the personality of the child kind of shallow; it could be different from day to day. Because of this, it is important to re-member that the personality reading that you were doing one day might be different the next day. This is not because you are reading wrong; it is simply because children change often and can be difficult to read.

With that being said, speed reading children is still somewhat similar to what you do when you speed read adults. You still need to look for their personality traits. For example, you can look to see if they enjoy spending time around other children or adults or if they prefer to spend time alone playing in their bedroom. These could be early signs that the child is either introverted or extroverted.

A highly sensitive person might not be noticed as highly sensitive when they are a child because almost all children are very sensitive. Children are still learning their emotions, so many of them have large emotional meltdowns and breakdowns often. This does not mean that they are highly sensitive or that they will be highly sensitive as an adult. Children also are easily offended. This is because they have not yet had the life experience that tells them they do not need to be offended by the words of the people around them. This is a skill that you learn as you grow up. Children might become easily irritated as well, but this is also not because they at highly sensitive people. This is simply because they have not yet gained the patience needed to not be irritated by the things that people are doing or saying around them.

How they receive and give love are easier to tell in a child than the other personality traits. Telling a child's love category is almost as easy as telling how an adult gives and receives love. The only difference is that an adult can usually tell you what they like best and that you will probably just need to watch for signs in a child instead of asking them to use their words to explain this complex topic. For example, if a child prefers quality time, they might constantly ask you to play with them. If they lean toward receiving gifts, they might be the happiest child in the world on Christmas or on their birthday, even more than other children seem to be. If they feel most loved through physical touch, they might be a big cuddler even as they get older and older. If their love is words of affirmation, they might behave better and perform better at their tasks if they are told they are doing a good job by the people that they love. If the child's love category is acts of service, they might act best after you help them clean their room or after you cut their waffle into little bites for them.

Some of the personality traits that we discussed for grown-ups might be more difficult to tell and children. For example, many personality types might be too complex to tell about in the young minds. However, the personality traits that we have mentioned in this chapter so far are easy to tell in children. This makes them good things to use if you're trying to speed read a young person.

Overall, we can tell that speed reading children is possible and learning their personality traits can be helpful. The things that we have to remember is that it is important to know those personality traits that are shown by children one day might change the next. You need to know that this change is normal because personality is affected by the things that we go through in life and it is changed by the person that we consider ourselves to be as well as the person that we aim to be. We also need to remember that reading the personality traits of a child can be difficult, especially if they are not yet talking or if they are not yet talking well. Even though these things can be difficult, we know that they are very helpful. If you know of the personality traits of the children in your life, you will better be able to help them with the things that they need. It might even make them feel loved in ways that they have not felt love before. Speed reading can be a good tool for parents as well as anyone who deals with children regularly.

Chapter 19: How To Personality Types To Your Advantage

You are learning how to speed read people for a reason. That reason is probably not only so that you can help the people around you. This can be a good thing to do, but you probably have some reasons that are a little bit more selfish. Luckily, it is easy to use speed reading for your own advantage. When you know personality types and traits, you will be able to use your knowledge to help you in many ways in your own life.

First, let's look into how you can use personality types and traits to get to know people better in your own life. If you need friends or if you are looking to start a new romantic relationship, you will be able to use your knowledge of personality traits and types in this journey. You will be able to tell the personality of the person whom you are trying to get to know, and you will be able to impress them because you will know what they like and what they need from you.

Next, let's look into how you can use your knowledge of personality types and traits to your advantage in your employment. First, you can use your knowledge to get you a job that you like. You can use it in your interview and your screening process and also use your knowledge when you have a permanent job to get to know your coworkers and work well with them. You can even use your knowledge to get to know your boss and impress them by doing the things that they like. This might even help you to get raises or promotions at work.

Knowing your personality traits and types can even help you in your home life. If you know the personalities of the people that are in your family, you will be able to love them better and help them better in what they need. This will, in turn, make for a better family solution for you. Your family will be happier, and you will have less stress in your home if you are able to give them what they need.

I remember growing up in a larger family. There were siblings, cousins, aunts and uncles everywhere. Someone was always coming and going.

But despite all of us being related, none of us seemed to have the same personality type.

I couldn't go up and talk to Uncle Tom the same way as I could cousin Suzy. They were different people with different personality types! Understanding this from a young age and learning how to read these personality types and get along with them helped me to have some of the strong relationships with my loved ones that I enjoy today.

You can use your skills in speed reading in places like the grocery store. If you are able to speed read your cashier, for example, and tell what type of personality they have, you might be able to get them to help you in a kind and polite way even if they are having a hard day. This is because you will be able to make them feel good about themselves and make them feel appreciated. In turn, you will not have to deal with workers that are not happy to help you.

If you know your own personality type, you can use them for your own good as well. You can use these personality traits to determine what type of worker who you are and use this information to get yourself the job that you would like best. If you know your personality type, you will know what type of job you will succeed in as well as what type of job you will enjoy.

If you know that you are a highly sensitive person, it will help you to know the reason behind why you react so strongly to certain situations. There's nothing wrong with being highly sensitive, but people might judge you for it. If you know that you have this straight, you can start feeling bad about the people that judge you for it. It will help you to understand that it is a good thing and that is a part of who you are.

Being highly sensitive is a gift that others might not fully understand. Many times, the most sensitive people I have encountered are the most trustworthy, the most caring, and the most likely to be there when you need them.

One time I had an acquaintance that I had met at a party. I remember being told to watch out when talking to this person, because they tended to take things to heart and feel under attack when the conversation started to get a little heated. With this in mind, I carefully steered the conversation away from anything that could be offensive or cause issues.

Later on, when I needed some help with finding someone to watch our beloved family pet when we had to leave out of town unexpectedly, they were the first ones to offer. They understood the situation, didn't feel like we were taking advantage of them, and had a heart of gold to be willing to help!

This is a good lesson on learning to be open to all kinds of people. You never know what they have gone through, and they can definitely be there for you, even when it seems unlikely!

If you know how you receive love, you will be able to help other people love you well by telling them what you prefer. This will help you to feel their love, and it will help the people around you to know how to show their love to you. They have it, so they might as well show it to you in the way that you can hear the best.

Overall, knowing personality types and traits can help your life in many ways. It can give you the ability to know the people around you, it can provide you with great life experiences, and it can help you to know yourself. It is a tool that everyone should know how to use.

Understanding the personality types of those around you, whether they are acquaintances or someone you are close to, can make a difference on how strong that relationship can be. For this exercise, take some time to answer the questions below to help open your views on how the personality traits of someone else can make their worldview different from your own.

How do you think knowing the personality type of someone else, and how they respond to the world, would change how you view them and some of their actions?

Do you think that if someone knew how you give and receive love or what you saw as an important way to express yourself, they would see you in a different light?

Chapter 20: How To Use the Meanings of These Traits To Your Advantage

We have already learned about the different personality types and traits and how they can help you in your life personally. Next, let's look into why you need to know as many little details as you can possibly memorize. These little details will help you to be set apart from other speed readers. They will also be able to help you no more information than just the basics when you are reading into a person's personality. The added benefits not only help you to read the people around you, but they can help you to better your own personal situation as well.

For example, if you don't know how to tell if a person is an introvert or an extrovert, you pretty much only know that they like to spend time in groups and they're outgoing or they like to spend time alone and that they are shy. However, if you know that they have many more characteristics because of those introversion or extroversion and you know what those characteristics are, you will know much more about the person you are read-ing.

If you know that extroverts also tend to like to be the center of attention, you will know that if you talk to them about themselves, it will make them happy. You can use this information in many ways. For example, you can use this information when you are talking to a person that you would like to work for someday. If you know that this person is an extrovert, you can talk to them about who they are and how you love everything that they have accomplished in their professional life. They will likely tell you more about themselves, and they will feel appreciated and heard. They will like that you want to learn more about them. This will make you stand out as a candidate for a future job, and it could get you the job that you would love someday. It could be the thing that sets you apart from others applying for the same job.

Another example would be if you know a person is an introvert and you want to go on a date with him. If he is shy, you could talk to him because you know that he probably won't be comfortable coming up to talk to you. You could also do most of the talking and ask questions to provide him with ways to talk back to you. You would also be able to know that he needs some personal space sometimes, so you would need to give that to him when he needs it and not be offended that he does not want to talk to you. If you notice these things about the person that you want to date, they will likely feel loved. They might even feel more appreciated than they ever had with anyone else that they had dated in the past. This would make you stand out as a person whom they could date, and it would make them possibly even want to go out with you more.

These two examples are two of many different ways that knowing the small details of personality types and traits can help you in ways that benefit your own life. Knowing who the person is inside and out from speed reading them not only allows you to better impress them and interact with them but also helps you get what you want from them. This makes it a good skill for you to have because it helps you personally in many ways of your life. In my lifetime, I have been fortunate enough to run across many different types of people. This has been a blessing and has helped me to learn how to speed read a bunch of different personality types.

Working with extroverts is going to be different than working with an introvert, for example. When it comes to an extrovert, talking about them and centering the conversation around social events and different outings have worked well for me. For example, talking about a recent concert they have been to allows them to explore their passion of being out with others and gives them a chance to talk about themselves, a winning formula!

The introvert, on the other hand, might not really like to talk about themselves. But this doesn't mean that they won't like to have some recognition as well. You just might need to bring them out of their shell a bit more.

I have found with introverts that taking control over the situation and being the one in charge is going to make a difference. It puts them at ease a bit more when they don't have to worry about coming up with all the topics, and you will find that they can be very agreeable communicators. One trick I have utilized is finding out some accomplishment of theirs, no matter how small, and giving a little praise with it. This can do wonders for helping the introvert feel noticed, and since they aren't likely to mention it themselves or fish for praise, it can really help them to form an attachment to you.

The more you can glean about a person from your speed reading, the more refined you can make your approach to talking with them. This will especially prove helpful when you encounter someone with a seemingly conflicting personality type. As an example, let's look at one of my patients, Tom, who was seeing me for help with anxiety and depression. When Tom first came into my office, my initial speed reading showed me that he was an introvert. He did not really talk much at first, and he seemed to be uncomfortable with making eye contact. As a result, I assumed that the best approach for getting him to open up would be for me to do most of the talking, at least for the first session.

This technique worked to an extent. Tom started talking little by little so long as I started the conversation, but in general, he still was not saying too much outside of brief answers to my questions. It seemed impossible to get him out of his shell. Then, during our third session, I noticed that he talked more than normal when I asked him what he was going to be doing that weekend, detailing a big woodworking project that he wanted to get started if he could just get himself to get out of bed. He even talked about how his family used to love getting homemade wooden gifts from him, back before his depression and anxiety had taken over. Seeing him become more animated with this topic, I realized that even though Tom was an introvert, he was probably also an intuitive. He clearly loved to dream and be creative as well as be appreciated for his creativity.

With this new information, I switched tactics a bit and started asking him about his dreams, his creative hobbies, and what he wanted in the future. Even though most introverts will not open up so easily about such details, Tom became like an open book. As an intuitive, he loved talking about his future and everything he dreamed of doing once he felt better. I still had to start the conversation by talking a bit about myself, but whenever I incorporated anything creative into the session or helped him to plan his future, he was more than willing to take the reins. Thanks to these additional details that I learned about him through speed reading, I was able to guide Tom through this dark time in his life and help him learn to control his depression and anxiety so that he could return to his bright, idealistic, and creative future.

Do not assume that one personality trait or type will tell you the entire story about the person you are reading. It will give you something to start with and get a conversation going. However, the more traits or types that you can categorize someone as, the better picture you will have about that person's inner workings. From there, it will be easier to use the meanings of the traits to help you get along with—and perhaps form a bond with—that person.

One Last Reminder Before Conclusion

Have you grabbed your free resource?

A lot of information has been covered in this book. As previously shared, I've created a simple mind map that you can use *right away* to easily understand, quickly recall and readily use what you've learned in this book.

If you've not grabbed it...

Click Here To Get Your Free Resource

Alternatively, here's the link:

https://viebooks.club/freeresourcemind-mapforspeedreadingpeople

Your Free Resource Is Waiting..

Get Your Free Resource Now!

Conclusion

Speed reading people is a skill that will serve you well your whole life. There are many different types of people in our world, and not all of them are going to react and see things the same way that you do. This guidebook has provided you with the insights and information that you need to finally be able to connect with anyone you meet, even if they prove to have entirely different personalities from your own.

I hope that after reading this book, you feel ready to speed read the people around you. I know that you now have all the tools, tips, and tricks that you will need in order to be successful in this process. Remember, though, that this is not a skill that you will be able to master overnight. Anything that is worth doing is worth doing well, and anything worth doing well requires practice. You cannot be an expert on speed reading people just from reading this book, but if you work at the techniques and using the tools that I have given you, you will become one.

If, for any reason, you feel like you need some more information to help you with speed reading or you would like to learn even more about the topic, consider reading through my book *How to Read Body Language.* Body language is just as important for speed reading as everything covered in detail here, so you will want the advantage of familiarizing yourself with this work as well. It is filled with just as much information as this book and will be able to help you with your speed reading as well.

I am thankful that you chose my book to use when you wanted to learn about speed reading. With this information, you will be ready for any type of challenge that comes your way. Your personal life, your work life, and even your romantic life will benefit from the new skills you have learned. Good luck on your journey!

Sincerely,

Harvey Augustus

P.S.

If you've found this book helpful in any way, a review on Amazon is greatly appreciated.

This means a lot to me, and I'll be extremely grateful.

More Books By Harvey Augustus

How to Read Body Language: Secrets to Analyzing & Speed Reading People Like a Book – How to Understand & Talk to Any Person (Nonverbal Communication Training Mastery to Improve Your Social Skills)

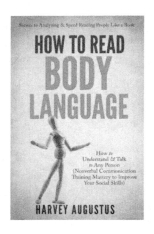

<u>Decode The Hidden Secrets Of Body Language</u> - Understand Exactly What Each Person is Saying, Feeling & Conveying With Their Body!

Have you ever wanted to understand what exactly someone is hiding or spot when they're lying just like a professional CIA agent?

Do you feel like you don't understand someone just to figure out days later what they actually wanted to say?

Have you been in a situation where you speak with someone and even though it all seems well you feel there's something a bit off about them?

Well, let me tell you...
Probably you weren't wrong, you just had no idea what exactly to look for.

If you want to stop all these in your life, and start analyzing and speed reading people just by looking at their body language and nonverbal cues, then keep reading...

Imagine this, you go to a party, business meeting, or you just met someone new. In less than 3 seconds you already know more about them than anyone around. You know if they're stressed, overwhelmed, or happy. You even know how they feel about you and every other person around.

More than that... Because nonverbal communication is 93% of what we convey, you're fully aware of how your nonverbal cues affect people. You understand your own body. You know how to make yourself likable. You feel limitless with your personal and social skills.

This could be your new REALITY!

Harvey Augustus has achieved mastery in the field of nonverbal communication with his decades of experience in body language. He combines the latest scientifically proven researches and decades of field-tested methodologies in his new masterpiece work.

***How to Read Body Language*, the only book you'll ever need to understand what everyone's body is saying.**

Here's a taste of what you'll discover inside *How To Read Body Language*:

- What body language actually is and how it influences the subconscious mind

- The latest scientifically proven researches on body language that will open your eyes

- Bulletproof method that experts use to detect if someone is lying or telling the truth

- Street-smart knowledge that accurately tells a person's feelings without words

- An effective way that will establish your leadership, dominance and influence instantly

- How to make someone trust you in just 5 seconds using only your body

- A quick and simple exercise you can do anywhere to boost your positivity in under a minute

And much, much more...

If you're ready to finally improve your people skills and become the person that everyone feels like they've known for years and want to talk to even if they've just met you, now is the time.

Made in the USA
Coppell, TX
27 February 2021

50964765R00105